Public Speaking for Beginners

An Effective Guide to Overcome Fear and Anxiety and Help You Build Your Speaking Confidence at Work, School, and Social Events

Cameron Wills

© Copyright 2020 - All rights reserved.

The content contained within this book may not be reproduced, duplicated or transmitted without direct written permission from the author or the publisher.

Under no circumstances will any blame or legal responsibility be held against the publisher, or author, for any damages, reparation, or monetary loss due to the information contained within this book, either directly or indirectly.

Legal Notice:

This book is copyright protected. It is only for personal use. You cannot amend, distribute, sell, use, quote or paraphrase any part, or the content within this book, without the consent of the author or publisher.

Disclaimer Notice:

Please note the information contained within this document is for educational and entertainment purposes only. All effort has been executed to present accurate, up to date, reliable, complete information. No warranties of any kind are declared or implied. Readers acknowledge that the author is not engaged in the rendering of legal, financial, medical or professional advice. The content within this book has been derived from various sources. Please consult a licensed professional before attempting any techniques outlined in this book.

By reading this document, the reader agrees that under no circumstances is the author responsible for any losses, direct or indirect, that are incurred as a result of the use of the information contained within this document, including, but not limited to, errors, omissions, or inaccuracies.

Table of Contents

Introduction 1
A Brief History 5

Part 1: Developing Your Voice 10

Chapter 1: 11

How to Find Your Voice 11
Introspection 12
How Do You Find Your Voice Physiologically? 18

Chapter 2: 25

Let's Get You Out of Your Comfort Zone 25
Defining Your Zone 27
Strategies for Stepping Outside of Your Comfort Zone 30

Chapter 3: 39

Time to Build Your Confidence 39
The Science Behind Confidence 41
Useful Strategies for Building Confidence 44

Part 2: Overcoming Fear 54

Chapter 4: 55

How to Overcome Fear, Anxiety, and Stage Fright 55
Why Do We Experience Fear and Anxiety When Speaking in Public? 56
Strategies to Overcome Fear, Anxiety, and Stage Fright 61

Part 3: Structuring and Delivering Your Speech 72

Chapter 5: 73

How to Organize Your Speech... 73

  How to Format a Captivating Speech.............................. 74
    What to Avoid..81

Chapter 6: 91

How to Prepare Speeches for Different Settings 91

  In the Workplace.. 91
    At School.. 100

Chapter 7: 116

Tips on What to Do Before and After Your Speech 116

  Helpful Exercises to Prepare You for Your Speech...... 117
    What Happens When It's over? 126

Chapter 8: 131

How to Effectively Deliver Your Speech 131

  Verbal and Non-Verbal Communication........................ 132
    Dress for the Part... 147

Part 4: Keeping Your Presentation Interesting 152

Chapter 9: 153

How to Use Technology to Boost Your Presentation Skills 153

  What Is Out There?... 154
    How to Keep Your Presentation Interesting........... 159

Chapter 10: 166

Public Speaking Pioneers..166

What Can We Learn and How Do We Implement Our New-Found Knowledge? *169*

Conclusion 173

References 180

Introduction

The stage is bare. The sounds of your heart beats are like footsteps running home to safety. You squint as the blindingly bright stage light moves over your head and stops to illuminate your entire being. You feel a bead of sweat drip down the side of your head as you try to conceal your shaking hands. Your face is flushed and your palms are sweating. You are acutely aware of hundreds of eager eyes focused on you as you try to push out the first words of your speech. Your legs are numb. You can't feel your fingertips. Your tongue feels like a giant, swollen gummy bear. You breathe faster and harder as you try to process what is happening around you. You are frozen.

If this sounds familiar, then this book is for you. Public speaking can be intimidating and sometimes debilitating for most people, which is why I am here to show you otherwise. You might protest that public speaking is not for you and it will never be. You may even be willing to die on this hill. I am also here to tell you that public speaking *is* for you. I will not only show you how you can overcome your crippling fear and anxiety around public speaking, but I will also turn you into a captivating and eloquent presenter. We will tackle the entire process of speech giving and presenting in its entirety, starting at the beginning with finding your voice, preparing for a speech, and stepping outside of your comfort zone. Once you have mastered these steps, I will show you how to deliver appropriate and successful presentations at work, school, and social events while highlighting the importance of contextualizing your speeches. But what about when it's over? Fear not, because we will cover how to answer questions after your presentation and supply you with the necessary strategies and tips for staying motivated and driven on your public speaking journey.

But first, what is public speaking? Well, it is exactly what it claims to be; speaking in front of an audience. Now, this audience can be two people or two thousand people, but it does not really matter because public speaking is the transference of information from you to your audience. Public speaking has become a widely researched and developed art form because to be a strong public speaker, you have to take a complex, multi-faceted, and holistic approach to presenting. To be successful, one must present and communicate effectively. Take yourself as an example. Are you particularly inclined to listen to someone who is presenting in a monotone, dry voice while talking about accounting? Probably not. But if this person were to stand in front of you, excited and eager, with an informative and to-the-point presentation, you would probably perk up and listen. This is why public speaking is so important; because communicating effectively means that people will listen to you. After all, if you are passionate about something, you will want the audience to share in your knowledge and excitement, but if you cannot communicate that efficiently, then you may find yourself alone in your belief.

Effective communication is especially important in the digital age because people's attention spans are shorter.

We read a quick article and if it takes us more than three minutes, we move onto the next one. We scroll through images and information like we are in a 100 meter sprint and the urge to stay updated and informed can be paralyzing. Nonetheless, this way of living has allowed the world to develop at an exponential rate and without this growth, we may still be writing letters to each other and sending them via snail mail.

We lead busy lives. We work, travel, and socialize and we simply do not have the time, attention span or desire to listen to a three-hour political rant. Perhaps the Greeks and Romans, or even people in the early 20th century, could sit and listen to speeches for hours, but today's society is different. We do not want fluff, and we do not have the time to beat around the bush. We want to be entertained and we want to receive the information that was promised to us.

So, why is it important to be able to communicate at work, school, and social gatherings? Well, effective communication is always important and necessary, but it is particularly beneficial to be able to get your message across in these spaces. For example, being able to deliver an informative and motivational presentation at work could lead to your next promotion. If you are engaging with your colleagues and superiors insightfully, making use of technology to improve your presentation, and keeping people interested, then you can expect an appropriate reward. This is especially important if your line of work requires you to work with clients. Effective communication contributes to a streamlined process for your customers which will inevitably boost their return on investment. What about at school? The same applies there. Often, group work and presentations are required to pass your modules and a good presentation can make the difference between an average grade and an outstanding one. The transference of knowledge is an integral part of your high school and college careers and being able to communicate your ideas to a group of people can be a superpower. It may even get you that A+ you've been pining after!

The necessity for public speaking at work and school makes sense professionally and with regard to our careers, but how do social events fit in? It might seem easy to speak in front of people you know, but you probably know that this is not absolutely true all of the time, purely based on your Uncle Bob's failed speech at your cousin's wedding last year. You also know that your contribution could make or break an event. Public speaking at gatherings and functions can be a great honor, but they can also end in disaster, which is why you need to make sure you have the skills and expertise to successfully execute a great speech. You might also be asked to speak at a social gathering for work, i.e., a fundraiser or gala, and in this case, there would be a lot more pressure. Either way, preparing yourself to make a speech correctly and tailor it to a specific setting will always be beneficial to you and your audience.

While context is important, many other factors need to be taken into consideration in order to deliver a successful and captivating speech. For one, body language is a crucial element of public speaking. If you show up hunched over and with your arms crossed, the prospects of anyone taking you seriously are very slim. If your body language is closed off and defensive, it will show the audience that you may not be confident in what you are saying. If you stand up straight, project your voice, and use hand gestures to enliven your presentation, the audience will have the confidence to trust you and will listen to what you have to say.

It does not end at body language either. You will also have to present yourself appropriately so that the audience can take you seriously. Remember, public speaking is about getting people to truly listen to you. To do that, you have to deliver your presentation honestly, openly, and effectively and I am going to teach you exactly how to do that. But first, let's discuss how public speaking became such an important part of our society.

A Brief History

Let me take you back to Ancient Greece. I am sure you have heard of Socrates, Plato, and Aristotle, the most influential philosophers of our time, but did you know that they started their journeys with public speaking? They did not have television or radio or newspapers to pass information on, but instead, they had their voices. These philosophers referred to public speaking as rhetoric and many of them used this art form to communicate political and philosophical ideas to the people of Greece. Socrates was even arrested and put to death for his influence on the youth!

Essentially, rhetoric is about persuasion and evidently, Socrates was a pretty great persuader. The actual theory of rhetoric was assembled by Aristotle. He divided it into three elements:

1. *Ethos*: This refers to the credibility of the speaker. If you, as a speaker, give false or misleading information, then the audience can no longer trust you. *Ethos* is concerned with the morality of the speaker. The more trustworthy you are, the more inclined people are to listen to you.
2. *Logos*: This explains how your speech is organized. It involves logic and rationality. Logos asks whether your speech makes sense. If it does not, then you have no foot to stand on and neither does your presentation.
3. *Pathos*: This deals with human emotion. How many times have you watched an advertisement for a sporting brand and walked away with goosebumps? The advertiser plays on your emotions to get a reaction out of you and similarly, speeches are intended to do the same for the audience.

So, the Greeks had a pretty good understanding of what public speaking was and how to use it to their advantage but the Romans took it even further. They divided rhetoric into five elements and started distinguishing between content and delivery. Cicero, one of the pioneers of rhetoric in the Roman Republic, stated:

> "The perfect orator should be able to speak wisely and eloquently on any subject with a dignified, restrained delivery" (DeCaro, 2011).

Therefore, public speaking, to the Romans, was not only about what was said, but how it was said. Quintilian, another Roman educator, noted five elements to rhetoric which he labeled as invention, disposition, style, memorization, and delivery. These elements have come to influence how we perceive public speaking today.

After the Greeks and Romans, public speaking dwindled in popularity due to the heavy influence of religion in the West. People no longer needed to be persuaded because they embraced the same belief system. But, with the Renaissance and the reintroduction of secularism, people soon began expressing their views again and public speaking once again gained traction. During the Renaissance period, people were divided by rationalist and humanist thinking which meant that they were still skeptical of public speaking. The humanists believed that public speaking could give insight into the human condition and the rationalists believed that only scientific explanations could do this. Eventually, with the emergence of political parties and democracy, public speaking came back with a vengeance and hasn't left since.

The Enlightenment was a period of human progression. After years of struggling and grappling with opposing ideals and ideologies, the Western world accepted reason as its fearless leader. People were thinking about and actively discussing philosophy, art, politics, literature, and with this, came the rebirth of public speaking. As democracies started to form, political parties were established and they needed a way to get their points across. So, political parties took to addressing their nations and started campaigning their ideologies in the hopes of being elected. In a non-political sense, the platform that public speaking created meant that people could share their knowledge of subjects such as art and philosophy. This exchange of ideas and opinions sparked the popularity of the art movement and without public speaking, we would not have a diverse and complex understanding of the arts today.

The largely political nature of public speaking during the Enlightenment is also what has formed our modern-day notion of public speaking; however, inventions like radio and television have created a nuanced and varied understanding of the art form. With the introduction of radio, speakers were required to be eloquent, to use the right language, and be entertaining to capture the attention of their audience with only their voices. However, when the television came into existence, speakers realized that they had to pay attention to non-verbal communication and body language as well. Merely standing in front of the camera and speaking would no longer be sufficient to keep listeners tuned in.

As we see it today in the 21st Century, our online presence has become a significant feature of our existence. The use of social media has us constantly displaying ourselves in front of an audience. We have opinions and instead of standing on a rock in front of our village, we write them down, attach a graphic image or video, and post them for the world to see. We even have online concerts and movie screenings that we can watch from the comfort of our own homes. If you are in school or working, you might have attended a few online meetings, and you may have given a presentation on a conference call. Just because it is online, does not mean that you can ignore the importance of preparing, delivering, and executing an interesting and charismatic presentation. Public speaking is evolving and so is the way we communicate with one another, but the basic fact remains that we have to communicate effectively and efficiently, no matter which medium is involved.

This book will not only show you the basics of public speaking, but it will provide insight into how the world has changed and how we can change with it. You might not be physically standing on a stage in front of hundreds of people. You might be huddled in your bedroom wearing a blazer and pajama bottoms, but the pressure is still on. Perhaps you have read some information on public speaking and were left wondering, *well, I know how to physically stand in front of an audience and give my presentation, but what do I do about my video call presentation in an hour?* Don't worry, because I have got you covered. Whether you have to give presentations in front of a boardroom full of people or from your bed, at the end of this book you will have all of the skills you will need to deliver an eloquent, unique and captivating speech. But let's not get ahead of ourselves! First, we have to find your voice.

Part 1: Developing Your Voice

Chapter 1:

How to Find Your Voice

Everyone has a unique voice and bringing it to the table is what could set you apart from the masses. While you may want to sound like Morgan Freeman or Meryl Streep, those voices are already taken. One reason for their success is not because they changed their voices, but because they enhanced them. Your voice is unique and if you use it to sound like other people, you may never know what truly sets you apart, and that would be a great shame. By reading this chapter and following the tips and tricks included, you will learn how to enhance your voice and begin sounding confident and comfortable. But how can you enhance your voice if you don't even know what it is yet?

This may be the most intimidating part of the process, which is why we have to start with it. Without a solid basis to start your public speaking journey, you may find yourself confused and unsure as you progress. If you are constantly worried about keeping up a persona, then other, more important aspects of public speaking may fall behind. The most important part of public speaking is to communicate effectively with your audience and if you are pretending to be someone you are not, then the audience will see through this. Remember when the Greeks were studying the philosophy of Ethos? The same concept applies here. If you do not stay true to yourself, the audience may not consider you to be a credible source. If you cannot be considered as a credible or authentic source, then the effectiveness of your communication becomes null and void and you may find yourself back at square one. Plus, it seems like a lot of effort to try to be someone else, no? Some people like to come up with alter egos when performing or presenting and this may be beneficial for overcoming fear and anxiety, but remember to make sure that your alter ego is still you—because at the end of the day, it is.

Finding your voice is going to demand introspection. No, you won't have to figure out your entire life's purpose or comprehend the true meaning of existence before you can sit comfortably with yourself, but you will have to reconsider a few things. This chapter will help you to find your voice and maintain it. As I said, starting with a solid foundation will allow you to focus on the nitty-gritty of public speaking without having to worry about pretense.

Introspection

Introspection is about looking inward to find out more about yourself, but that's not all it is. You have to actively analyze and decipher what you come to find out. It is simple to say, *I don't like public speaking because I'm shy.* Anyone can do that. It's easy to put limits on ourselves and our personalities when something feels a little too uncomfortable, but without discomfort, there can be no growth. View this chapter as growing pains or the shedding of skin. To become a better version of yourself, you will have to let go of your misconceptions and limitations. Sometimes, it can be difficult and drawn out and you may have to change some aspects of yourself. If you want to be a successful public speaker, I am calling upon you to challenge yourself; not just when you are speaking, but always.

With most introspective exercises, we have to start with the "who, what, and why." It might seem like a tall order to answer all of these questions and I am not demanding you to have everything figured out. Some of these will be easier to answer a bit later in your journey and some may be more challenging. However, to start your journey, you must at least begin to consider these concepts.

So, let's start with the *who*. Who are you? We spend our lives trying to figure out who we are, trying to find definitive traits and characteristics that we can cling to. The truth is that humans are constantly evolving and changing and to limit ourselves to one way of being is against our natures. I am not suggesting that we change into entirely different people every few years, but our interests shift, our friends may change, and our environments will evolve. So, while it is necessary to have an understanding of who you are, it needn't be as strict as you think. Surprisingly, one of the most important places to start your journey will be by letting go of who you think you are and who you want to be. Let go of your preconceptions and prerogatives and start with a clean slate. Although, I am going to tell you to do the exact opposite in a second, the point is to start fresh.

Consider your life and start drawing a timeline, from birth to the present moment. Write down, for each year of your life (that you can remember), what you felt, how you viewed yourself, and the traits you felt were definitive to your being. From there, you can begin to see how you have changed, overcome, failed, and possibly stagnated. However, the main purpose of this exercise is to decipher who you think you are. Seeing a physical representation of the life you have lived and your state of being at each point will allow you to identify recurring and constant characteristics and traits. What stayed the same even when your environment changed? Which part of yourself remained as you started interacting with a new friend group? We want to differentiate trends from truth. Don't just stop at the timeline; make this an active part of your life. When you go to the coffee shop, are you the type of person to let someone in front of you because you don't know what you want yet, or do you keep the order of the line? Ask yourself what this says about your character. If you relate to the former example, then you may be a deeply empathetic and caring person. If you feel like the latter is more accurate, then perhaps you can classify yourself as someone who values justice and order? The point is to think about what your actions and thoughts say about you. Eventually, you will get to a point where you no longer have to analyze these encounters with yourself because you will just exist. You will be who you are without definition and analysis. At the end of the day, your experiences, the people you interacted with, and the decisions you made have shaped you day by day. This exercise will help you to identify that shape. You already are who you are.

Once you have started consciously considering who you are, you can move on to the *what* portion of introspection. What do you want? And no, I don't mean what do you want for lunch? I mean, what do you want out of life? What do you want to do, to become, to see, to embody, to say? While the *who* focuses on the past and present, the *what* focuses on the future. Public speaking is not just about speaking in front of an audience, it is also about having something to say and wanting to communicate that with people. As discussed in the earlier section, humans are changing and so are our desires, beliefs, and interests. Considering what you want to say is to be intentional with your motives and your voice. Later in the book, you will have an opportunity to consider what you want to say concerning a specific speech and context. For now, this is a general question and requires some "bigger picture" thinking. This element to finding your voice is specifically personal because everyone has different reasons and motivations for saying what they say. They also have different things to say based on their contexts and environments. Only you can answer this question and you might only figure it out halfway through your journey. Set your intentions, figure out what you believe in, and start linking that to who you are. Think of these three elements (who, what, and why) as a bullseye. The inner ring is who you are, the middle ring is what you want, and the outer ring is why you are the way you are. Make a mind map inside each of these rings; you can use keywords, sentences, bullet points, and pictures. A mind map is a type of diagram that allows you to map out your ideas. For example, a mind map starts with a main topic, and in this case you are considering what you want, which will act as the heading of your mind map. From there you can use bullet points, pictures or keywords to highlight the things you want. Using a mind map in this way will allow you not only to consider each ring individually, but also to view all of the rings as a whole. You will be able to start creating links between the three elements. Use this as your roadmap to finding your voice. This is only the start of your journey, and there is so much uncharted territory yet to be discovered.

Here's another question for you: *What about you is interesting*? What can you bring to the table that other people can't? Perhaps you excel in comedy, or you have a unique way of expressing your ideas. Maybe your body language is striking and interesting. The point of all of this is to figure yourself out and by doing this, you can discover what makes you different. Neil Gaiman, a prolific author, says, "The one thing that you have that nobody else has is you. Your voice, your mind, your story, your vision. So write and draw and build and play and dance and live as only you can." So, just by being yourself, you are already unique and different. Dig a little deeper, get to know yourself, and fulfill your true potential.

Now for the outer circle—the *why*. Don't worry, I am not asking you why humans exist. Quite frankly, no one knows why. But what I do mean is why do you want to say whatever it is you want to say? The outer ring is the ring of motive. Sure, you know who you are, and you know what you want to say, but for these elements to actually mean something, you have to ask yourself *why*. What is your motivation? Why is this important to you?

If what you want to say is not important to you, then your voice will lack the conviction necessary to fuel your success. Using your mind map is the perfect way to identify your motives. Ask why until you can't anymore, and expand your thoughts and ideas as much as possible on your mind map. Exhaust every possible cause, source, and catalyst. Don't just ask why speaking about endangered animals is important to you, figure out when in your life this became important to you, how did your upbringing have an effect on your present opinions, what made you aware of the issue of extinction. To be intentional, you have to ask *why*. These three elements will give you the foundation needed to find your voice and become a confident and comfortable public speaker.

When you have considered yourself and your motives extensively, it may be time to turn to the people around you. Sometimes, we can get caught up with our ideas about ourselves because we only ever see ourselves in a mirror or in photos. The people around you, your friends, family, and even acquaintances, see you as you don't see yourself, when you are not consciously aware of how you are acting and the way you come across. In this sense, it is valuable to see how they perceive you. You also do not have to take everything they say into consideration, but pick the good ideas and the ones you relate to and let them fuel you. Perhaps you will consider yourself an introvert until a few close friends start questioning this. You might realize that while you do enjoy solitude and need to recharge your "social batteries," you also really enjoy talking to and meeting new people. Your perception of yourself may be somewhat incorrect and limiting until the people around you point out your extroverted tendencies. Sometimes, we are too close and we fail to see the bigger picture. Getting some distance and third-party input can be helpful and transformative.

You might be wondering what finding yourself has to do with finding your voice, and the fact is that it has *everything* to do with finding your voice. To be self-assured and confident in public speaking, you have to know what you want to say and how you are going to say it and you can't do that without a little introspection—or a lot of introspection in this case. Finding your voice is about identifying your homeostasis. What about you stays the same even when your context changes? Your voice is a part of you that needs to remain constant and stable, despite your ever-changing surroundings.

How Do You Find Your Voice Physiologically?

This process is different for everyone and I am not saying you have to change your voice to be more charismatic or likable. Finding your true voice is about using what you have and making it better. After all, why sound like someone else when you can sound like yourself? For a better understanding of how to improve and curate our voices, we must first understand how the voice works.

The vocal process is made up of three parts; the respiratory system, the phonatory system, and the resonatory system (Ebersole, 2018). Each of these elements works together to produce sound. The resonatory system deals with your mouth, nasal passage, and throat. Think of it like a gramophone; the giant horn standing above the body is where the sound comes out. Just like this horn, our mouths, noses, and throats can project sound and form the words we speak. The phonatory system consists of the voice box and vocal cords. These elements create the vibrations required to make a sound. Like the gramophone, this is where the needle hits the record and sends sound up to be projected through the horn. Finally, the element holding these systems together—the respiratory system—refers to the breath, lungs, rib cage, chest, and diaphragm. The breath moves up to the voice box which causes the vocal cords to vibrate which sends sound up to the mouth and nose to make the words you speak. The respiratory system acts as the crank that powers the movement of the record that comes into contact with the needle and sends sound up to the horn.

The vocal cords are two muscles that lie opposite each other. When air from the lungs flows through these muscles, they separate to create a hole in between them. Basically, the vocal cords are like a pressure valve. If there is no steam in the valve, it will remain closed. However, as soon as the steam snakes up to the top of the valve, it opens up to release the steam to prevent implosion. Similarly, when the pressure of the air from your lungs becomes too much, the chords open up and release air to the resonatory system which releases this air as sound due to vibrations.

What is interesting about vocal cords is that they are, in fact, muscles and muscles can be trained. This is why understanding how the voice works can be beneficial to your journey. It might feel hopeless and futile in the beginning, but if you persevere, you will soon notice changes in your conversational flow and tone.

How to Fine-tune Your Voice

So, you now know how the voice works, but now we have to delve into how you can enhance it. There are a few simple ways you can begin to train your vocal muscles so that you can speak in a manner that comes naturally to you. The goal is to sound confident, comfortable, and effortless. The following helpful and effective strategies will give you everything you need to start sounding like your true self.

1. Practice, practice, practice!

You're going to be hearing this throughout the book, but that's because it is an essential part of your public speaking journey. The more you practice, the more comfortable you will start to feel about your voice. It might feel strange in the beginning because you will actually be paying attention to what you sound like for the first time in your life. As you get more comfortable, you will be able to see (and hear) your progress. Set aside some time for yourself every day and start a ritual, similarly to how you might get up in the morning and make yourself a cup of coffee. Wake up, make that coffee, and do some vocal exercises. All you need is 15 minutes a day to get those vocal cords working and sounding right.

2. Find your breath

Is it lost? Where did it go? Don't worry, it is right where it has always been, but it has probably been a little neglected. Our busy lives make it difficult to remember to breathe fully and deeply and if you have ever been to a yoga class, then you will know what I'm talking about. All of that deep and intentional breathing might even have left you feeling light-headed and dizzy after the class! This is because we live in a world of confinement. We wear tight clothes, sit at desks for hours, drive to and from work in small cars, and breathe in polluted air. Our breath has generally become shallow and throaty. Finding your voice is about using all of the space in your lungs to breathe—from the bottom to the top. Creating a full and deep breath will allow you to control your voice and the air that moves through the phonatory system. It is essential that this eventually becomes an unconscious action, but for now, make sure to consciously breathe deeper and slower and maybe go to a yoga class or two.

3. Speak from the diaphragm

It sounds a little obtuse; what is a diaphragm anyway? It is the muscle at the end of your rib cage. When you get the hiccups, that's your diaphragm in spasm. So, how do you access this elusive muscle? How do you breathe and speak through your diaphragm? You don't. You breathe through your lungs. However, to "breathe" through your diaphragm, you will need to fill up the bottom of your lungs with air. Try pushing your stomach out without breathing. Great, now inhale and push your belly out. It's as easy as that! Making your breath slower and deeper will allow the air coming from your lungs to flow seamlessly through the rest of your body until it gets to your mouth and throat.

This goes hand in hand with posture. If you are hunched over, then it is physically more difficult for your vocal cords to let air through to your resonatory system. Exercising your voice is not just going to be about doing vocal exercises. It might also mean having to strengthen your entire body to create open channels of communication between the three vocal systems. The better your posture, the easier your breath can flow from your lungs to your vocal cords to your mouth.

4. Record yourself

This might be your worst nightmare, but it is an incredibly helpful and pertinent step to finding your voice. After all, the point is to be happy with the recording eventually, so you will have to start somewhere! Record yourself alone in a room. Sometimes, it is easy to sound different or to use a slightly different accent when speaking in front of people. Play the recording back to yourself and make notes of the elements you like and dislike. Keep in mind that you aren't trying to change your voice, but merely enhance and strengthen it. Maybe you noticed that your breathing is a bit shallow or your tone a bit too nasal, and make sure to note this. Now, record your voice several more times, each time finding a different projection. For instance, record yourself speaking from your throat; open it in one recording, and close it in another. You can also make a recording of your voice when it is a bit more nasal. Find the most comfortable and audibly pleasing method and start to practice with it. Record yourself every few days to see if you can notice any changes.

5. Find role models

As I said at the beginning of this chapter, there is no point in trying to sound like someone else. However, this does not mean that you cannot draw inspiration from good public speakers to enhance your own voice. Find someone with a similar pitch to yours and analyze how they speak and breath. Do they take shallow breaths? Do they speak through their diaphragm, nose, throat, or mouth? By finding someone with a similar pitch to yours, you will not be tempted to completely change your pitch and tone, but will be able to learn and adapt from your observations. You will also want to maintain realistic expectations for yourself. If you are trying to model your voice after famous film actor Jack Nicholson, for example, you might have a hard time trying to replicate his deep, raspy voice. It is best to avoid disappointment from the onset.

6. Practice mindfulness

This is a crucial step to finding your voice because practicing mindfulness involves being present. Being present means that you are only focused on your current existence at that exact time. This requires that you are not thinking about the past, future, what people might think of you, or how you should act. Therefore, in a truly present state of mind, you can begin to figure out who you are just by existing. After all of the introspection and self-analysis, mindfulness can bring everything you have learned about yourself into fruition. On a subconscious level, your mind will begin to process everything you have mapped out and these concepts, thoughts, feelings, and desires can start to blossom. Mindfulness will give you the space to actualize the who, what, and why of it all and soon, you will be on your way to giving the best presentation of your life.

Take a second, make yourself a cup of tea, draw up some mind maps, and get to know yourself. We tend to take things for granted in this life and we stop paying attention to what we actually want, who we are, and even how we breathe. So, let's nail the basics and start on a firm foundation. Finding your voice will make your public speaking journey so much more productive and fulfilling.

Chapter 2:

Let's Get You Out of Your Comfort Zone

I know. It's warm and snuggly and full of safety in your comfort zone. You don't have to try too hard and failure is but a speck on the horizon of your bubble-wrapped existence. Why would anyone want to leave it? The truth of the matter is that the world would be a lot less developed if everyone stayed in their comfort zones. Imagine if Elon Musk decided not to invest in the development of eco-friendly cars. Maybe we don't see the full impact of his efforts currently, but the environment will thank us for it later. What if humans stopped trying to develop earthquake-resistant buildings? We might still be rebuilding our houses on a yearly basis. What if we decided that space travel was not for us and we would rather be confined to Earth forever? You can't build a hovercraft from your bed and realistically, nothing worth doing has ever been easy. So get up, put some pants on, and let's get you out of your comfort zone!

This may be obvious, but defining our comfort zones can help us to effectively break away from them. A comfort zone is an invisible barrier that is created to keep ourselves safe. It is a method of preserving ourselves. Think of yourself as a preserved fig in a jar. If you stay in that jar, you will always just be a preserved fig, not contributing to anything, not creating anything. However, if you venture outside of that jar, you could end up on a deliciously crisp piece of toasted sourdough bread with a slice of brie and a rasher of bacon. You could be transformed into the *pièce de résistance* of the entire appetizer, the spirit of the whole dish, the element bringing balance to the delicacy. Stepping outside of your comfort zone means that great things can happen.

Similarly, if you don't go bungee jumping, then you probably won't end up falling to your death. However, the logic of the safety of the comfort zone is flawed in two ways. Firstly, just because you won't die by falling to your death while bungee jumping does not mean that you are immune to any unfortunate events occurring. Terrible things still happen to people even when they are in their beds, or going to the grocery store. Secondly, while bungee jumping may be a terrifying experience, not doing it might mean missing incredible opportunities for growth. Putting yourself out there will most likely always lead to growth. I'm not saying something good will happen right away each time you step out of your comfort zone. Basically, you will win some, and lose some. But, on the ones that you do lose, you will walk away with a lesson. You will either win, learn, or both. Perhaps bungee jumping is an extreme example, so let's take a step back. Imagine Usain Bolt was too scared to talk to reporters after his race, so he decided never to try out for the Olympics. We would not have seen one of the greatest sprinters of our time run at the Olympics! Imagine Paul McCartney was too shy to sing in front of people. We would never have had The Beatles! Staying in your comfort zone may be holding you back and the sooner you step out, the sooner you will begin to experience exponential personal growth.

Defining Your Zone

Now that you know what a comfort zone is, we have to figure out what *your* comfort zone is. Just like in the previous chapter, we are going to have to go through a process of—you guessed it—introspection! I know it can be difficult to look inward, but we live in a world that is full of distraction and subterfuge. Before you know it, you're 80 years old, sitting on a porch, and unsure where your life has gone. Introspection offers an opportunity to be cognizant of yourself, your life, and the people around you. It gives you a chance to take everything in before life rushes past you. Plus, if we are going to define your comfort zone, then we are going to have to figure out what makes you tick. This is a very personal journey and there is no magic formula that can be applied to everyone. I can give you the tools and show you how to push your boundaries, but you have to decide for yourself what your boundaries are.

So, let's start at the beginning. To define your boundaries, we have to figure out where your limits are. Start by asking yourself what makes you comfortable and uncomfortable. Think back to when you were at school. Did you like to sit at the back of the class? Were you comfortable answering questions? Did you begin to feel uncomfortable when the teacher asked you a question? In this context, we can say that your comfort zone was largely defined by your interactions with others. Perhaps you were the most comfortable when the teacher did not ask you to speak in front of the class and also when you did not have to participate in group work. Ask yourself this: *If you had participated in group work and made a friend, would the discomfort have been worth it?* Only you can answer this, but I think most people would reply with a sincere *yes.* Were you reluctant to ask questions even though you didn't understand a topic? Perhaps if you had asked that question, you might have gotten a higher grade instead of grappling with a challenging topic on your own.

Let's take it into the workspace. Do you enjoy interacting with your colleagues? Did you ever have a great idea, but declined to share it with your superiors for fear of failure? Your comfort zone could be the thing stopping you from getting that promotion or collaborating with that impressive colleague in the office next to yours.

What about in a social setting? Do you walk up to people and introduce yourself? Are you eager to get to know people? I am not telling you to entirely change your personality; however, as humans, we have put limits on ourselves without even realizing it. We limit who we can talk to, what we can say, and how we can be, just because we have preconceived ideas about ourselves and are afraid to fail. The sooner you realize that the prospect of failure and embarrassment is going to be with you for the rest of your life, the sooner you can begin to move forward from the shackles of fear.

So, how do you begin to define what makes you comfortable or uncomfortable? I like to picture a circle around myself, like a literal zone or boundary. I put all of the comfortable things in the circle with me and all of the uncomfortable things just outside of this boundary. As you begin to push your boundaries, try to physically picture yourself stepping outside of them. Once you have completed something that makes you uncomfortable you can begin to expand your boundary. Now, I'm not saying that you have to entirely do away with your comfort zone. Some things you just do not want to do, and that's okay. But how do you stop yourself from thinking of everything outside of your comfort zone in that same way?

Here's how: You make a hierarchy. Make a list of everything you are afraid to do, do not want to do, dread doing and/or simply cannot ever imagine doing. Then, draw a pyramid and divide it into three sections. Each section will represent a different level of discomfort, starting with the least uncomfortable to the most. It might look something like this:

> Kind of uncomfortable: Eating lunch alone at a restaurant, telling the waiter they got your order wrong, or asking an acquaintance to hang out for the first time.
>
> Relatively uncomfortable: Public speaking, making a suggestion at work, or answering a question in class.
>
> Incredibly uncomfortable: Bungee jumping, performing in a play, or asking someone on a date.

Public speaking could be placed into any one of these sections, as your journey is personal and you get to decide the level of comfort or discomfort you would feel. This hierarchy of discomfort will allow you to decide which tasks to tackle first, which ones may need a little more time and which ones you might need a lot more time to incorporate. As you go through the items on your lists, make another diagram, kind of like the bullseye you made in Chapter 1. Make one circle on the page and put all of your comforts in there. As you cross off each uncomfortable thing you have completed, you can start to add more rings around your original circle of comfort. Before you know it, you will need another page for all of the rings you have added. But how do you actually move outside of your comfort zone?

Strategies for Stepping Outside of Your Comfort Zone

1. Start small

Sometimes we get excited and we want to dive headfirst into whatever we are doing. It's like when you have a big school assignment and you go to the stationery store and buy a basket-full of amazing paints, pens, and stickers. You rush home, excited and motivated and suddenly, a few days later, you find yourself procrastinating and forcing yourself to complete the task. Going hard and fast can lead to a quick burnout.

Starting slow and small will ensure that you succeed in your first few attempts to push yourself out of your comfort zone. If you start with the most uncomfortable task on your list, the chances of failure are very high. You want to maintain your motivation in the beginning by giving yourself small wins, just to prove to yourself that you can do it, you can break these boundaries. Starting small will also make the physical act of starting far easier. You will not likely go to the gym and lift the first 100-pound weight you see. You would start with 10 pounds and work your way up. Breaking out of your comfort zone works in the same way. Slow and steady wins the race, after all.

2. Doomsday theory

Let's say you want to take on a relatively uncomfortable task today and that task is speaking in front of your class or at your workplace. The doomsday theory asks: *What is the worst thing that could happen?* What is the worst thing that could happen when you give your presentation? Perhaps you jumble up your words. Maybe you move through the slides too quickly and get a little lost. What if you forget what to say and people laugh at you? None of these things are so bad that you wouldn't be able to recover from the failure or embarrassment.

Picturing the worst-case scenario will not only allow you to be prepared for it, but it will also minimize your fear of stepping outside of your comfort zone. Being able to identify the worst-case scenario can put your mind at ease because the worst thing that could happen is often not even that bad. Sure, you could slip up and say the wrong thing and maybe end up feeling a little embarrassed, but is that really so bad?

3. Change up your routine

Comfort zones are about predictability and routine. If you know what is going to happen at every stage and you have control over what happens, then you can remain snug and guarded in the little zone you have created for yourself. Therefore, bringing some spontaneity into your daily life will disrupt the loop you are stuck in. Additionally, making yourself aware of change and the effect it may have on you can also prepare you to deal with more unexpected and abrupt changes. Instead of going on your morning jog, brewing a nice cup of coffee with milk and two sugars, reading the news on your phone, and getting in your car to go to work, try something new. Try waking up, doing a pre-run yoga workout, going out to buy a coffee (or perhaps one of those Frappuccinos, just to spice things up a little), and then reading the newspaper before you walk to work. Whatever your routine, try to find ways to change it up. Remember to start slow and then completely tip it on its head. You might even end up enjoying it.

4. Breathe through the discomfort

As you read this book, I will supply you with several breathing exercises that can be used for anxiety, warm-ups, and exercises. You can refer back to them as you come across them, but for now, the important point of this strategy is to move through your discomfort. Be uncomfortable and do it anyway. Breaking the boundaries of your comfort zone will be challenging and you might find yourself tempted to get out of achieving a few of the goals you have set for yourself. This is a call to action not to back out. Even though your legs are shaking and your palms are sweating, breathe through the discomfort and fear. I promise you will come out on the other side as a better version of yourself, but for that to happen, you have to actually do it.

5. Talk to strangers

For some people, this is their worst nightmare. It might even be yours. Nonetheless, it is an incredibly useful skill to learn, especially on your public speaking journey. Talking to strangers will not only drive you outside of your comfort zone kicking and screaming, but it will also give you the skills needed to deliver a smooth and confident presentation or speech.

Whether you are at work, at a social event, or at school, there will be people who you don't know. Walk up to them and start interacting. The worst thing that can happen is that you learn something new and interesting about someone. You may even make a friend or two! You don't know what to say? Remember to start small. Ask them about the weather, find a common interest, and learn how to pitch to them. Remember how we talked about finding what you want to say in Chapter 1? Well, that should help you with finding things that are important to you. Talk about those things. Talking to strangers will teach you a lot about other people and yourself, and trust me, it will get easier. That's the point after all, to make those uncomfortable things, comfortable.

6. Say yes

Did you ever watch that movie, *Yes Man* (2008)? Jim Carrey plays the main character and the premise of the movie is that his character has to say yes to everything. I know everything kind of blows up in his face towards the climax of the film; however, he does walk away with a ton of new experiences, a girlfriend, an amazing job, and a solid group of friends. Most of the time his character struggles with saying yes, but once he starts, it comes quite naturally to him. If you don't put yourself out there, you'll never know what could happen.

It's almost like Sylvia Plath's metaphor of the fig tree. In her story, she finds a beautiful fig tree and all of the figs look so beautiful, ripe, and sweet that she can't decide which one she wants. Eventually, plagued by indecision, the figs began to fall to the ground and rot. That is what can happen when you stay in your comfort zone. All of the opportunities outside of your comfort zone could begin to rot and fall away before you even have the chance to grab hold of them. Don't wait, say yes, pick the first fig you see, and it will be great. And who knows, you may even have time to pick another one.

7. Read more

Your lifestyle may not lend itself to reading more, but I am not asking you to pick up War and Peace by Tolstoy. I am, however, asking you to read material that you think you might have no interest in. Read some articles and stories that you might not be initially inclined to read. Broaden your scope of interest, read a few academic theories, and read outside of your culture. Learning new things will not only give you more to speak about, but it will also subconsciously push you to want to know more, see more, and understand more. The hunger for knowledge and experience can be something that forces you out of your comfort zone in a healthy and exciting way.

8. Interact with risk-takers

This is really going to get you out of your comfort zone. Having someone to motivate and push you is always going to get you further than you can get by yourself. It's easy to get stuck in your ways, but having someone disrupt your way of thinking and cause some havoc can be just the reset your mind needs.

Interacting with risk-takers not only allows you to try new things, it also allows you to see how easy it can be to try new things. You may see others fail, but perhaps the difference between them and you is how they handle the failure. Observing how other people cope with things may motivate you to not take your discomforts so seriously.

It is also helpful to have a support structure. Surrounding yourself with people who have taken risks, failed, and succeeded will allow you to learn from them. It also means that if you freak out a little, they could guide you through the discomfort.

9. No more excuses

This is easier said than done. It's easy to say, *Oh well, I have had a really tough week and I don't think I should be partaking in any uncomfortable tasks right now. I'm just going to sit in my bed and scroll through my phone; nice and safe.* Unfortunately, that is not going to work. Getting out of your comfort zone is going to require you to identify when you are making excuses for yourself. When you know you are making an excuse, shut it down. This may also be a result of a lack of motivation. Look back at your hierarchy of discomfort diagram and pick something small to do; something you know you will be able to succeed at. Get yourself out of that comfortable bed and out of that comfort zone. There will be some days when you aren't going to be motivated, but you will have to work through this and remain dedicated. The fire isn't always going to be there, but you can't keep making excuses for its absence if you want to succeed.

10. Positive mantras

It might feel silly to say positive mantras to yourself, but they can be an effective tool in building your confidence and affirming that you are capable of stepping out of your comfort zone. Your effective mantras may sound something like:

- I can do this.
- I am strong, capable, and fearless.
- I believe in myself and my abilities.
- I am proud of myself for trying.

This is dependent on your preferences and what you think might work best. You may even want to include some phrases that apply directly to your character:

- I am a strong leader.
- I care deeply for others.
- I am a good person and I want the best for people.

Don't just stop at positive phrases. Tell yourself why you are a good leader or how you care deeply for others. Sometimes, getting out of your comfort zones means being gentle with yourself. If you feel positive, comfortable, and confident, the chances of success are far higher.

11. Failure is part of the journey

Similarly to the doomsday theory, failure is rarely as bad as we think it might be. Accepting failure as part of your journey will allow you to learn and grow. Do you think when the Wright brothers were inventing the first aircraft they did not fail a few times? Sure, they failed, but if they didn't keep going, then we would not be able to fly to France for our summer vacation. What about space travel? We wouldn't have incredible photos of earth from outer space if we didn't keep trying. So, don't see failure as a dead-end street, view it as an intersection, and as a road that presents more opportunity.

You might not relate to all of these strategies and you will have to gauge them in relation to your hierarchy of discomfort diagram. Just remember that stepping out of your comfort zone won't be easy, but it will be necessary. If you find yourself struggling, slow it down, backtrack, and try to revisit some of your less uncomfortable tasks. This journey is unique to you and you can do it at your own pace and in your own way, but don't fall back into your comfort zone again. Remember to push yourself and your boundaries.

A great way to keep yourself on the right track is to set up a list of goals. These can be dependent, once again, on your hierarchy of discomfort diagram. This hierarchy will also allow you to keep track of what your next goals should be. Tick those goals off your list and move on to the next ones. Try not to stagnate and if you do, don't be too hard on yourself. You will be surprised what you can accomplish with a little motivation.

Chapter 3:

Time to Build Your Confidence

Confidence refers to the belief we have in our skills and abilities. When we are confident about something, we are certain that we will succeed. It seems straightforward, no? You just have to believe in yourself and you will be confident. Unfortunately, it doesn't quite work like that. Depending on your context, environment, upbringing, and level of self-esteem, confidence can be quite a hard thing to come by. Unlike a tattoo, it is not permanent. Confidence can wax and wane as we move through different stages of our lives. It is not something acquired once and suddenly, you're set for life. Confidence is something you have to work at, even when you do feel confident. Things can change, tasks can get more challenging, or you might start to feel intimidated. You may be a little out of your depth in certain situations and it is in those times where confidence will be the most difficult to conjure, but also the most necessary.

It is important to know that self-esteem and self-confidence are two different concepts. While they are closely linked, self-esteem refers to the general outlook and positive feelings and perceptions we have of ourselves. If you have high self-esteem, then you will most likely be a confident individual. However, if you experience feelings of incompetence, guilt, shyness, and unworthiness towards yourself, then the chances of you believing in your capabilities are slim. It is difficult to feel confident if you do not have a positive perception of yourself. Therefore, this chapter will show you how to build your self-esteem as well as your confidence. You can't confidently walk into a room full of people if you don't believe in yourself. However, you can have high self-esteem and still struggle with confidence. This may be due to the environment you are in. Perhaps you view yourself in a positive manner, but you do not have enough experience to believe in your abilities yet. Self-esteem and confidence are not mutually exclusive. Either way, I will provide you with helpful strategies to get you feeling confident and assured.

Having confidence is particularly important to your success in public speaking. Have you ever been in a lecture hall and it was quite clear that the lecturer did not want to be there? He was hunched over, facing away from the class and never made eye contact with his students. You could barely hear him and you spent the entire lesson copying your friend's notes to try to get an idea of what he was saying. That is not a very effective way of giving a lecture and it is especially unproductive for the students. Not only that, but because he lacked the self-confidence to stand in front of the class and teach his students, he was unable to communicate his message. That is why confidence is such a significant aspect of public speaking. If you believe in what you are saying and in your ability to effectively communicate it, then your audience will listen to you. Let's say you made an astounding discovery in your field and you have to give a lecture to your colleagues. If you do not have any conviction or any confidence, then it won't very much matter that your discovery could change the world as we know it.

However, confidence can feel like quite a vague subject. We don't really know how to predict it or curate it. If we did, then everyone could always be confident! Sometimes, our belief in ourselves and our capabilities can be hit or miss and we don't really know what changes from one day to the next. In a world full of confusion, I am here to give you some structure and a deeper understanding about confidence. Understanding how something works takes the unknown out of the equation and not knowing is one of humanity's greatest predicaments.

The Science Behind Confidence

I would like to give you a full rundown of exactly what happens to the brain when one begins to feel confident or unconfident. Unfortunately, research has only now started gaining some traction in the field. Confidence is still somewhat of an enigma. Something that makes one person feel confident may make another feel incapable and unmotivated. Therefore, we cannot say for sure that one specific experience or act can boost the confidence of humanity. Although, we can get more insight on the topic, even if we don't discover a magic formula. An exciting experiment with rats has allowed us to understand that confidence is something that can be created. It is not a strange, unattainable nebula that floats through us, but a set of chemical reactions in the brain.

Because humans and rats have very similar brain structures, scientists are able to conduct in-depth experiments with rats as subjects to find out more about the human brain. The scientists at Cold Spring Harbor Laboratory in New York were able to determine that rats experienced surges in confidence and that their confidence could be measured mathematically (Castillo, 2014). They performed two tests on the rats. The first test involved releasing an odor behind one of two doors. The rats had to choose which door was producing the odor. The second test involved the rats having to pick the most dominant odor out of several different scents. The scientists found that the rats were willing to take their time to make these decisions. By making a hasty decision, they were more likely to choose the incorrect door, but by waiting, their chances of success were greater. As the rats gained confidence in their decisions, the amount of time they took to decide which door and which odor was correct had lessened. Thus, the scientists could measure when the rats became more confident and how much more confident they were likely to be after succeeding. This same concept can be applied to humans. When we have more confidence in our abilities, we do not spend time second-guessing ourselves or making sure that we have made the right decision because we already know that we have. For example, if you are making a chocolate cake that you have made 100 times before, then you will probably be able to finish it quite quickly. You know the recipe, you understand the method, and you know it's a great-tasting cake. However, if you start making chocolate ganache tart with raspberry tuile and a hazelnut praline, you will probably take a long time to finish it. This is because you don't know the ingredients, the order, or the techniques, and you have never made it before. So, to make up for your lack of knowledge, you will compensate with extra time and attention.

In another study, led by Dr. Aurelio Cortese in Japan, they discovered that they could predict confidence in individuals. They also found that the brain can be manipulated into a state of confidence (Whiteman, 2016). Dr. Cortese's team tested a target group of 17 people while they were performing perceptual exercises. The exercises involved visual perception games, such as finding a specific object on a page, or completing a picture, or connecting the dots. By monitoring the brain during the activities, the scientists were able to identify when the individuals were experiencing high or low levels of confidence. In this sense, confidence is closely linked to the brain's reward system. As soon as an individual was able to successfully complete a task, an increase in their confidence could be seen.

The interesting part is that the team tracked the brain's chemical reaction to the influx of confidence and established what happened to the brain in a state of low confidence versus high confidence. By doing this, they could target the necessary brain centers to induce confidence. The team set up a session in which they gave the participants a small monetary reward when they were feeling confident. This differed from a standard reward system in which the subject completes a task and is rewarded for it. This experiment does not reward success, but confidence. The participants did not realize that they were being rewarded for their levels of confidence instead of their task completion abilities. The scientists were, therefore, able to subconsciously curate confidence. According to Dr. Cortese himself, the results of the experiment were that "when the participants had to rate their confidence in the perceptual tasks at the end of the training, they were consistently more confident" (Whiteman, 2016).

From this experiment, we can also link the brain's reward system to feelings of confidence. According to Deborah Halber, author of *Motivation: Why You Do the Things You Do* (2018), humans are fueled by two things: necessities and rewards. The brain's reward system can be found in the striatum which deals with motor functions and rewards. Basically, neurons are activated and release dopamine when we expect success or a reward of some kind (Halber, 2018). This is why confidence makes us feel good; because it involves dopamine and other happiness hormones. Additionally, this confirms that confidence is not necessarily about the reward or success itself, but rather our perception of success in relation to the belief we have in our abilities. So, to an extent, we can track human confidence and we can manipulate it, but how does that get us to a point where we truly feel confident?

Useful Strategies for Building Confidence

A good place to start would be to decide when you feel your most confident and when you feel the least confident. This will help you to decipher what you can do on your personal journey to feel better and more assured. We know that confidence is a reward-based system, but because it is so closely linked to self-esteem, we can figure out when we subjectively feel our best. For instance, perhaps you feel most confident while wearing your blue blazer, or when you have just gotten a haircut, or completed a high-intensity workout. These stimulators are different for everyone and figuring out what yours are can help you to maintain and nourish your confidence. Building confidence can be quite challenging, especially when you think of it in terms of public speaking. This chapter will give you insight on how to improve your overall confidence as well as your speaking confidence. Now that I encouraged you to step out of your comfort zone, I have to show you how to feel good about it!

1. Be positive

This is easier said than done, but similarly to propping yourself up with positive mantras, a positive outlook on life can have wonderful effects on your confidence. Being positive is about changing your mindset. Say, for instance, on your way to a holiday house, you hit something sharp while you are driving and you have to stop to change your tire. On one hand, you could play the victim and wonder why this inconvenient thing happened to you, cursing and scoffing at every corner. You get into the car and your mood is soured for the rest of the day, you can't even enjoy a nice dinner at your destination. You hyped yourself up so unnecessarily that what started as mild annoyance became full-blown contempt for the world around you.

Instead of falling deeper and deeper into a pit of unhappiness, let's say you take the time to change your tire and while doing so, appreciate the view around you. If you were driving, you would not have been able to take in the mountainous terrain and golden sunset. Now you can calmly drive to your holiday house and begin your week of relaxation. Doesn't that sound a lot nicer?

It is easy to get caught up in bad things that happen to us. Terrible things are constantly happening around us and we are often so high-strung that even the slightest inconvenience can set us off. Being positive is an active and conscious decision to see the good, even when there isn't a lot of it. Being positive will help you to handle failure in a way that does not paralyze you, but makes you grateful for the opportunity. It is also healthier for you and your mental health to maintain a positive attitude which will, in turn, contribute to feelings of higher self-esteem.

2. Be prepared

Confidence is about believing in your skills and capabilities, so if you are prepared and knowledgeable, then you will have nothing to worry about. If you are going into an exam and you forget all of your equipment, would you be walking in there confidently? Probably not. You might be distracted and annoyed that you forgot essential equipment. However, if you have studied hard, made sure you had everything you needed and double-checked yourself, you would be able to walk into that room, chest puffed out, pencil at the ready, and write that test to the best of your ability.

The same goes for public speaking. The Romans considered *memory* to be an element of public speaking and they did so with good reason. If you know your speech, then you can walk in front of that audience confidently and calmly. This is not a vague step that will work for only a few people. If you want to be confident in your abilities, then you have to be prepared. Even if you don't feel confident, being prepared means that you can communicate your message and, just like the rats, the more times you get it right, the more confidence you will have.

3. Don't search for external affirmation

When we search for external affirmation and approval from others, we make ourselves susceptible to failure. If our perceptions of ourselves are based solely on outside opinion, then we can never be happy. Someone will always have something negative to say and not everyone is going to like you. To base your self-worth on an unpredictable and fallible foundation is to set yourself up for future failure. Yes, external validation can be beneficial, but getting all of your confidence from outside makes believing in your own abilities impossible. Confidence is not about whether other people believe in you, it's about whether you believe in yourself.

When you find strength, affirmation and validation within yourself, you are creating a stable and safe environment to be who you are. Building this foundation can help with your self-esteem and confidence because it means you are not confined to other people's opinions. Mark Twain said, "A man cannot be comfortable without his own approval" and he was exactly right. If you cannot accept yourself, then how can you expect anyone else to? Don't let your fate rest on anyone's shoulders but your own.

4. Be present

Similarly to how mindfulness can help you to find your voice, being present can help you with your confidence. If confidence has to do with your ability, then being able to focus, in that moment, on your presentation will block out everything else that is causing you to be unconfident. Instead of worrying about what people will think and say, or whether you will make a mistake, all you have to think about is saying what you came to say. Worrying about things that you can't control or that haven't happened yet will distract you from your ultimate goal of communicating effectively.

5. Make a timeline

Just like the timeline you made when you were tracking your comfort zone, making a timeline for your confidence can also be beneficial. Think of yourself as a scientist observing confidence trends in test patients (mainly yourself). Set up a timeline of your life and write down at which points you felt most confident or not confident. Perhaps in your final year of university you were handing in assignments on time, getting A's, and feeling confident in your abilities. Write that down and figure out what the driving force was. Maybe the very next year when you started working at a new firm, your confidence dropped as you noticed a gap between your knowledge and what was expected of you. Figure out what you could have done differently. What was your outlook on life like? How was your self-esteem? Did you get yourself out of that rut? Figuring out how you deal with these situations will allow you to create a tailored strategy for times when you may begin to feel less confident.

6. Change the way you view failure

This is similar to changing your mindset to view things more positively. We often default to the idea of failure as a dead-end street. Failure means no more options, no more attempts; it's kind of like the death of something. However, failure can be a really beautiful, helpful, and necessary step to success. Failure prompts us to think outside of the box. It's like finding the perfect recipe to bake the best chocolate cake. The first recipe you try is good, but a little dense and not chocolatey enough, so you add some cocoa and make sure your whisked eggs are fluffy. Now, your cake is chocolatey and fluffy, but not moist enough, so instead of milk, you use buttermilk. Failure challenges your brain to think of solutions. If you didn't keep trying recipes and learning from your mistakes, you would not have created a reliable and delicious chocolate cake recipe. Failure is not a limitation, but quite the opposite. It opens up doors and teaches you how to overcome challenges. So, don't shy away from failure, but embrace it, call to it, and let failure make you a better person.

7. Fake it 'til you make it

Sometimes, pretending to be confident and then succeeding can be just as effective as actually being confident. You just need a little push in the right direction to prove to yourself that you can do it and you can be sure of your abilities. So, stand up straight, don't cross your arms, breathe through your diaphragm, speak loud and proud, and pretend as if you know what you're doing. The audience won't know the difference.

8. Find someone to learn from

Role models are a great way to learn things. When finding your voice, it is slightly more challenging to copy and mimic your role model because you don't actually want to be someone else. However, confidence is a universal language and watching someone strut onto a stage with confidence and conviction can help you to figure out how to portray that same level of assertiveness. Watch how they carry themselves, how they talk, and where they put their hands. What does their body language look like? Do they forget what they are trying to say or is their message clear, concise, and to the point? Make notes and try to emulate their confident demeanor while adding your own unique twist. If you're faking it 'til you make it, this is a great exercise to learn how confident people interact with their audience.

9. Reward yourself

This is a more scientific strategy to boost your confidence. Remember that experiment I mentioned; the one where they gave the participants a reward when they were feeling confident? I know, the whole point of this exercise is that the participants are somewhat unaware of when they are feeling confident. However, if you reward yourself every time you succeed or feel a little boost of confidence, you can essentially train yourself to feel more and more confident in yourself and your abilities.

10. Take care of your body

Make sure you get some exercise, eat healthily, and make your mental health a priority. Exercising releases serotonin (the happiness molecule) into your brain which means that exercising can literally make you happier. Dopamine and serotonin make up the best happiness cocktail and feeling good about yourself involves boosting that self-esteem. You don't have to turn into a fitness junkie or become a vegan. Exercising for 30 minutes a few times a week will do wonders for your mind. Also, taking care of yourself indicates that you value your life and your existence and that is one of the core factors of building self-esteem—the realization that you are worth it.

Making sure your mental health is stable is also an important facet of increasing confidence because low self-esteem is often a result of feeling alone, unworthy, incapable, unimportant, and insignificant. Monitoring your brain's patterns and emotions will allow you to take more control of your life. Go to see a therapist, download a calming app, or speak to your friends and family. Make sure you have a solid support structure who will listen to you when you need it.

11. Visualize success

The way dopamine works is that it is released in anticipation of a reward. So, obtaining the reward is not actually what induces dopamine. Therefore, visualizing success can be instrumental in chemically increasing your level of confidence. Remember how the striatum works? Dopamine is released upon the expectation of success when you are feeling confident (because if you are not confident, you probably aren't expecting to be successful). Visualizing success allows you to manipulate your mind into mimicking confidence. Nifty trick, isn't it?

12. Let go of things that no longer serve you

Mature, grown-up conversations are difficult. Friends and family who are toxic are challenging to deal with. Holding on to the past is damaging. When I say let go of things that no longer serve you, what I mean is to have the confidence to live without them. It feels contradictory. To gain confidence, you have to let go, but to let go, you have to already be confident. You have a point, but that's not exactly what I mean. It is a process. Cutting people and objects out of your life is going to be challenging; however, it is essential to the development of your self-esteem and confidence. Sometimes, we shy away from having that difficult conversation, or telling someone they no longer have a place in our lives. If you want to improve your situation, you are going to have to bite the bullet. Taking charge of your own life and deciding what serves you allows you to put yourself first. Similarly to how exercising and eating healthily shows that you care about yourself and your well-being. Letting go of things that do not serve you is also a form of self-care and puts you one step closer to living a confident and happy life.

It may seem like a tall order. Feeling confident and assured can feel like a giant speed bump in your public speaking journey. However, the process of finding your voice and pushing yourself out of your comfort zone will give you the necessary tools to appreciate your capabilities. And if all else fails, remember to be prepared, and fake it 'til you make it!

Part 2: Overcoming Fear

Chapter 4:

How to Overcome Fear, Anxiety, and Stage Fright

Even if you are confident and secure in your voice, public speaking can still be incredibly anxiety-inducing. There is always the "what if" that sits at the back of your mind. What if you make a mistake? What if no one laughs at your joke? What if you completely fall apart in front of everyone? While these things may very well happen, it is very unlikely. But that's the snag. It does not always have to be rational, or logical, or even a possibility. As soon as that seed of doubt is sewn, you're done for. Although, not completely because I am going to show you exactly how to deal with fear and anxiety. Fear is a little different because it can act as a driving force. When fear replaces reward or necessity, we can begin to crumble. Instead of staying on track and visualizing our success, we get stuck in an endless loop of negativity.

Overcoming fear, anxiety, and stage fright on your public speaking journey will be one of the most valuable lessons that you may take away from this book. If you can overcome your anxiety in front of a crowd, what would be stopping you from overcoming other adversity? In this chapter, we will look at the reasons for our fear and anxiety and how our brains handle these emotions. I will provide effective strategies for overcoming anxiety and when all else fails, there is a guide on what to do when you are in the throes of a panic attack. These tips and tricks can be applied to all moments in your life. Just like doing daily exercises and vocal warm-ups, keeping your anxiety at bay is going to take work and commitment.

Why Do We Experience Fear and Anxiety When Speaking in Public?

People experience fear and anxiety for different reasons. However, concerning public speaking, the list of reasons becomes a lot smaller. Sure, you might experience less impactful hang-ups, like if someone in the audience is wearing the same outfit as you or what if one of the stage lights falls on you, but these are highly unlikely events. While our subjective experiences of anxiety will all be different, the way our brains perceive the anxiety is quite similar. Public speaking anxiety is about the anticipation of fear. It is about thinking and fixating on every little thing that could go wrong. Quite naturally, when you see or think of a threat, you begin to prepare yourself to act against this threat. The stage fright you may experience is a result of the brain's ability to defend itself against danger. Essentially, the stage fright, anxiety, and fear around public speaking cause your body and mind to enter into survival mode—which seems crazy, when you put it like that. It's not like your life is being threatened. It's just speaking in front of an audience. Jerry Seinfeld famously questioned this phenomena stating:

> "According to most studies, people's number one fear is public speaking. Number two is death. Death is number two. Does that sound right? This means to the average person, if you go to a

funeral, you're better off in the casket than delivering the eulogy" (Saks, 2014).

In the grander scheme of life, public speaking is not that scary. Once we acknowledge our fear, we can stop giving it the power to control us. However, in these moments, if your brain perceives a threat, you will have one of three options: fight, flight, or freeze. Stage fright can manifest in any of these three ways but either way, your body is activating a stress response against an external threat.

When your body goes into any one of these three modes, your brain begins to release cortisol, otherwise known as the stress hormone, and adrenaline. The cortisol works to activate a *primal* response to the danger. Basically, your brain shuts down everything that is not necessary for survival at that point, including the hippocampus where your long-term memory is stored. That is why, when you get up on that stage to give your presentation, you might find yourself forgetting everything you prepared. Your brain does not care about the speech; it just wants to get you out of there alive!

John Daly, Professor of Communication Studies at the University of Texas, and his team believe that highly anxious people are more susceptible to stage fright because of their increased self-awareness (Daly, 1988). He posits that focusing on the self during public speaking leads to poorer performance than by non-anxious individuals. This is because it curbs the individual's ability to adapt and understand whether the audience is responding positively to the presentation. He also theorized that individuals with a high level of anxiety are encumbered by negative thoughts and emotions about themselves, thus adding to their anxiety and public speaking ability. Boosting confidence and stepping outside of your comfort zone can be healthy and effective ways to manage your anxiety. If you feel better about yourself, then you won't fall into the vicious cycle of self-deprecation.

Professor of Psychology, Maria Tillfors (2002) and her team did an experiment on a group of subjects to elucidate why people experience anxiety during public speaking and what effect this anxiety has on the brain. The participants were asked to deliver two speeches, one in front of an audience, and one alone in a room. They were required to have their eyes open for both of the exercises and their reactions were to be recorded. Tillfors found that the participants experienced anticipatory anxiety. In the same way that your brain may release dopamine in anticipation of a reward, your brain can also release cortisol in anticipation of a stressful event. They noted increased heart rates and subjective anxiety in the participants. They also found that repetition can lead to decreased anxiety. This is because the brain begins to understand what is happening. The same level of anxiety may not be experienced every time you give a speech because the thing that fuels your anxiety, a fear of the unknown, becomes less significant the more you expose yourself to it.

Apart from the chemical and physiological aspects of fear and anxiety, we still do not know why we are prone to having these extreme brain and body reactions when faced with the prospect of speaking in public. As I said, reasons may differ for everyone, but I have put together a list of three potential factors which may be driving your fear. Remember, anxiety is a symptom and manifestation of these fears. By identifying why we feel fear, we can begin to address its symptoms and effects.

Fear of failure

The world around us is outcome driven. We are so focused on productivity and mass production, that we forget life is more than just the number of hours we have worked, or the promotion one might get, or the money being earned. Yes, these aspects are important to life and they motivate us to keep progressing. But they don't need to consume us. In this way, fear of failure is based on output. If you are unable to give your presentation, then you will not have completed the task. Your superiors may be disappointed with this as you have now cost the company time and resources. However, this fear becomes crippling and prohibits you from completing the task anyway.

Another form of fear can take the shape of personal failure. No one likes to fail. Quite frankly, it sucks. But if you have started taking my advice from the previous chapter, then you will realize that by changing your perception of fear, you can eliminate the fear that propels you. Remember, failure is an opportunity, not a negative representation of your ability.

Losing control

Anxiety is your brain's way of desperately trying to maintain some semblance of control. Public speaking may feel like a loss of this control because it is. You are only in control of yourself and your presentation, not the people around you. This can be a source of stress for many people; however, once you realize you can't control anything else, it actually becomes easier. All you have to do is focus on the presentation and what you can control and let the rest happen as it will. You know that saying, *if you love something, let it go*? Sometimes we grasp onto things so tightly because we are afraid of not having them that we end up harming everyone in the process. We try to hold onto our sense of control so intensely that it ends up hurting us. Free yourself of the need to be in control and focus on your presentation.

Embarrassment

This is rooted in people's perception of you. What is contradictory about this is that it requires us to focus obsessively on ourselves, while being dependent on the approval of others. As with confidence, you cannot place importance on the opinions of others, not even positive opinions. Once we start believing the positive things people have to say about us, it can be easy to fall into the trap of listening to the negative things as well. Sure, it's nice to hear good things about yourself, but that cannot be the sole reason you feel good. That strength and positivity must come from within. The nice things people say about you are merely leaves on an already strong and stable tree.

People have different reasons for fearing embarrassment. Perhaps you experience abandonment issues and therefore associate embarrassment with rejection. This is specifically applicable to younger individuals who are still in school or who were bullied. We may hold these moments close to us for years after the trauma occurred. The fear of embarrassment is nothing to be ashamed of. It is just something you have to work through. Figure out why you have these feelings in the first place. Was it because of your school experiences? Perhaps you had negative encounters with friends or family? Either way, finding the root cause of your fear and anxiety will allow you to move forward in your public speaking journey. Yes, failure, embarrassment, and loss of control can seem like devastating possibilities, but in the grander scheme of things, they are not so bad.

Strategies to Overcome Fear, Anxiety, and Stage Fright

Because everyone's journey is so personal, it is important to analyze your individual journey. What makes you anxious about the whole process? Write down your fears and examine them. Get to the root of the problem. To cure something, you must first identify the cause. Your anxiety started somewhere. It manifested in a specific way and now you have to deal with it.

A lot can be said for exposure therapy, especially when treating anxiety. Exposure therapy is part of Cognitive Behavioral Therapy. It prompts you to do the things that make you anxious. The point is to increase your level of anxiety and allow your brain to find ways to deal with this anxiety. Similarly to how the rats gained confidence in the previous chapter and began taking less time to make correct decisions, your anxiety will begin to dissipate as you expose yourself to the very thing that terrifies you. Aside from therapy, here are a few useful tips and strategies for overcoming your fear, anxiety, and stage fright:

1. Picture everyone naked

Okay, not literally, but the point of this popular technique is to show that you do not have to take the presentation so seriously. You are allowed to take a light-hearted approach to your speech to help with your focus. Now, it is not so much about picturing everyone naked as it is about finding a spot to focus on, or maybe three evenly dispersed spots because staring at one person for the entire presentation might make them feel uncomfortable. Choose three focal points and refer back to these people throughout your presentation. This maintains engagement with your audience, but can also help to reduce your anxiety and stage fright. If you have chosen three focal points of people who make you feel more comfortable, then you can begin to put yourself at ease. There is no pressure to look at every single pair of eyes in the audience. All you have to do is present to those three people and you will be golden. If you don't want to look at people, you can choose focal points around the room, although do make sure they are close to the audience; or otherwise, you may appear disinterested or even more nervous than you already are.

2. Breathe

Maintaining a low and slow breathing rhythm won't only help you to speak through your diaphragm, but it will also calm your nerves. When feeling afraid or anxious, your body will take you into fight or flight mode. Either way, your body releases cortisol to activate a stress response to the situation you are in; public speaking, in this case. Cortisol mingles with adrenaline to create a stress response which leaves you with a racing heart, sweaty palms, and butterflies in your stomach. When this happens, your top priority should be to calm yourself by breathing deeply, calmly, and slowly. If you begin to breathe slowly, then your heart rate can calm down along with your brain. We often underestimate how exhausting stage fright and anxiety can be to our brains. Just getting some regulated oxygen and blood flow to your brain and body can already leave you feeling better. Breathing exercises are also a preventative method of curbing anxiety and fear. Breathing allows you to be mindful and to remain present in the moment without having to think of the *what-ifs*.

3. Practice and preparation

The more prepared you are, the more confident you will be in your abilities. You also won't have to question whether you know your presentation well enough, or whether you have practiced enough. Preparing ensures having one less thing to feel anxious about. It's true that even if you've prepared until you are blue in the face, you may still forget something or mess up, but that is part of the process. Be prepared, trust in your abilities, and learn from your mistakes.

Before your presentation, try to only go through your introduction and conclusion. Going through the entire speech may cause you to feel rushed and pressured. By focusing on a small part of your speech, you can maintain the order and intention with which you practiced.

    4. Scope out the situation

Anxiety involves worrying about the unknown, so trying to have as much information as you can will help ease you into your presentation. Go to the venue, figure out where you are going to stand, how much you can walk around, and where your audience will be sitting. If your presentation involves a PowerPoint show or uses technical aids, then find out if you have all of the necessary equipment. You don't want to have the most amazing presentation prepared only to find that you should have put it on a flash stick and not a memory card. Unpredictability is not your friend. Find out how many people you might be speaking to. There is a difference between fixating on the size of the audience and being mentally prepared for the audience. The more you know, the less you will have to worry about.

    5. Stop thinking

Easier said than done, I know. Especially when you have fear breathing down your neck and anxiety dripping down to your palms. This is where mindfulness comes into practice. If you try to ground yourself and focus only on the present moment, you will prevent the what-ifs from swirling around your brain. Stay focused, concentrate and don't think about the past, future, or the audience's opinion. Unless you are visualizing your success, the future can be your biggest setback and trigger. If you struggle with staying present, find a focal point to look at or try bringing awareness to different parts of your body. Concentrating on how your foot feels is far more calming than wondering which door you need to run out of after you bomb.

6. Perfection is not the goal

You've practiced your speech, you know every letter, every comma, every exclamation point, and the thought of it being any less than perfect is crippling. Unfortunately, that's not how it works. Humans are fallible and we make mistakes. Striving for perfection has misled us into thinking that it is attainable. It is not. So, walk into your presentation looking forward to your mistakes. If they don't teach you anything, they might still improve your speech. Maybe you change up the wording or add a pause where there should be a comma. Practicing alone in your room is different than actually giving a presentation. Sometimes, the audience is different than anticipated and you have to think on your feet and change up a joke. It is important to be adaptable and flexible. Getting rid of the expectation of perfection will allow you to walk onto that stage with a relaxed and confident mindset.

7. It's not about you

This may be a hard pill to swallow, but anxiety can often be a very self-absorbed emotion or condition. When we are anxious, we are worried about what could happen to us, not anyone else. In this way, if through the platform of public speaking, we can begin to be more selfless in our thoughts and actions, then our focus will shift from ourselves to the presentation or to the audience. This will allow you to separate yourself from the situation.

Being negatively consumed with ourselves can lead to toxic emotions, which in turn, can lead to our downfall. By focusing purely on the presentation at hand, you can ensure that you don't get in your own way. If you separate yourself from the success or failure of the presentation, then the fear of failure no longer needs to be a driving force in your motivation to give the presentation. I am not asking you to completely dissociate from the experience, but I am saying that you do not need to be at the centre of it. Sure, you are giving the presentation and people will be watching you, but at the end of the day, your main priority is to get your message across and to communicate with your audience. If your anxieties are stopping this from happening, then you may need to separate yourself from the situation. Distance makes the heart grow calmer.

8. You are not alone

While it may feel that way a lot of the time, especially when you are feeling anxious, it is important to remember that you, in fact, are not alone. As I said in the previous point, anxiety can make us seem and feel self-absorbed. You might think that no one can understand what you are feeling or maybe even that what you are feeling is invalid and silly. Neither of these things are true. The feelings of fear and anxiety are always valid and founded. The reason we try to treat these feelings is because they can be limiting and painful. While people may not understand your exact problem at that point in time, they can still offer valuable support. Try communicating with people about your needs. With all that newfound confidence, you will possess the necessary tools to have a mature conversation with the people around you about what your needs are. Feeling alone can leave us thinking like we have no safety net and no support system. These aspects are important to our general well-being. Humans are not meant to be alone, so stop trying to isolate yourself and ask for help when you need it.

9. Release the tension

This is a very effective way to get your blood flowing (in a good way) and get your mind off of your anxiety. When you feel anxious or fearful, you may notice your heart start to race, you may start sweating, your breathing getting faster, your pupils dilating. There is so much happening in your body that you have to release it, otherwise your body will release it for you in the shape of a panic attack. Depending on what you are comfortable with, you can start dancing, doing jumping jacks, engage in a few yoga poses, jog on the spot—whatever helps you to release that pent up energy. On top of that, moving around and exercising will release serotonin into your brain and body which means that you will physically feel better.

10. Keep going!

Whatever you do, don't give up. Things get hard and it can be easier to walk away than to put the effort in. Your public speaking journey is not going to be a smooth, linear line. There are going to be ups and downs and you're going to wish that you never had to speak to anyone ever again. Breathe through the frustration and anxiety to get back to your journey.

In a more literal sense, when dealing with anxiety, it is important to keep doing what you're doing. Working through the fear and anxiety and realizing that you are capable of giving a great presentation will help you to see that your anxiety can be treated and managed.

What to Do When You Are Having a Panic Attack

A panic attack is an intense reaction to a perceived threat. There are many different strategies for dealing with a panic attack, but the most important goal is to get you to calm down. Some people respond well to grounding exercises and others respond better to breathing patterns. You may have to go through a period of trial and error, but finding a coping mechanism is just as important as dealing with your anxiety head-on.

I am providing you with two methods to implement when you are having a panic attack. The first two exercises are part of the grounding method which aims to get you out of your brain and back into reality. This method will require you to focus on your senses and surroundings. The next two exercises are breathing exercises which aim to refocus your mind. Breathing will physically calm you down as well as distract you from your panic.

5-4-3-2-1 method

This method focuses on sensory stimulation. As explained by Psychologist and Author, Dr. Sarah Allen, there are five steps to this method:

- Name 5 things you can see
- Name 4 things you can feel
- Name 3 things you can hear
- Name 2 things you can smell
- Name 1 thing you can taste

You can do this exercise as many times as you want, each time thinking of new things to identify. Bringing you back to your surroundings and identifying your actual situation, instead of the unrealistic what-if situation will allow you to calmly reorganize your thoughts. Working through your anxiety, as opposed to running away from it, will show you that you are going to be okay. This is why repetition is useful, because we know nothing awful is going to happen and we can acclimate to our surroundings. However, if you don't work through your anxiety, you could very well be in a state of panic each time you have to speak in front of an audience.

Focus on one thing

Pick an object that comforts you. This could be a stone, keychain, picture, or coin; preferably something small that you can carry with you. When you are in the throes of a panic attack, you can grab hold of this item and focus entirely on it. Block out everything else around you and in your mind. Let's say you picked a coin. You can look for any imperfections in the ridges. What color is the coin? Where is the coin from? What is written on it? As you begin to ask and answer these questions, your mind will be able to refocus and recenter your thoughts away from your anxiety. Keep in mind that this is not an opportunity to ignore what caused the panic attack. Remember to treat the cause once the symptoms have subsided.

Alternate breathing

This breathing exercise requires you to alternate breathing between your left and right nostrils. Hold down your right nostril with your thumb and breathe in for six seconds. Breathe out for ten seconds and then switch nostrils. Do this as many times as necessary until you stop hyperventilating and feel your brain start to return to homeostasis.

Equal breathing

This breathing exercise is quite lenient in the sense that you can choose a time limit that suits you. I like to stick to breathing in for ten seconds and breathing out for ten seconds. This gives ample time to slow down the breath.

Counting to ten can also be soothing to allow your mind to focus on something other than your panic.

Fear and anxiety are challenging concepts to deal with. We can easily feel silly for having these emotions. It is only public speaking, after all. Not really. Public speaking can be grueling. Everyone's journey is different and everything you feel is valid. I am here to help you to find a healthy and productive way of dealing with your emotions so that you can excel. You have all of the strategies and tools you need to succeed—all you have to remember is that everything is going to be okay.

Part 3: Structuring and Delivering Your Speech

Chapter 5:
How to Organize Your Speech

Okay, you have found your voice, broken the boundaries of your comfort zone, embraced your confidence, and learned how to deal with fear and anxiety. Now, you have to learn how to write and organize a speech. This is important because it allows you to prepare appropriately for a presentation. As I have mentioned in the previous chapters, being prepared is paramount to your success in public speaking. Similarly, you cannot walk onto the stage with confidence if you do not know what you are going to say or how you are going to say it.

Organizing one's speech is not a modern concept. Remember when I mentioned the Romans and their philosophy of public speaking? They came up with five elements; invention, arrangement, style, memory, and delivery. Invention dealt with what to say. Arrangement was the order in which one would say these things. Style was the words used to say these things. Memory was remembering the things to say and delivery was the manner in which one would say them. Even though these elements were thought up thousands of years ago, we can still benefit from them. Many other things in our daily lives have changed, like buildings, efficient sewage systems, and even the internet has changed the way we communicate, but the fact that these elements remain true and applicable today, shows that public speaking is something that can be mastered. Not only that, but it is timeless. Even as we communicate through social media and video calls, communication and storytelling will always be part of human nature.

This chapter will help you to format a captivating speech, to understand the dos and don'ts of speech making and show you how storytelling can help you to win over your audience. We will take inspiration from the Romans as I show you how to organize your speech in a neat, effective, and interesting way. After all, you've got to showcase that new confidence of yours somehow!

How to Format a Captivating Speech

1. What, why, where, and how

Similarly to the Romans' exploration of invention, you have to decide what you are going to say. Different contexts will require different topics that we will discuss in the next chapter. For now, deciding what you want to say is the crucial first step to creating a successful speech. Therefore, we have to understand what, why, where, and how your presentation is going to take shape.

Firstly, what are you talking about? Let's say you are a personal trainer and have to give a speech at work about sport climbing. Are you going to be talking about the necessary safety precautions when climbing? Perhaps you can give an in-depth analysis of all the gear? You may want to go over some of the injuries that can be caused by climbing or give a detailed map of the safe and fun climbing spots in your local area. Topics can be very broad and it is your job to narrow down to exactly what you want to discuss and make sure it can be widely understood.

Why are you talking about climbing? Well, you are a personal trainer and therefore, sports fall under your area of expertise. You could be addressing your colleagues at the gym or perhaps a group of people who would like to take up climbing. Either way, make sure you are qualified to talk about the topic you are presenting. People want to walk away with more knowledge than they came with and it is your job to make that possible.

Knowing where and when your presentation is to take place can help you prepare fully. You may think knowing what you want to say and why you want to say it is sufficient, but to give a well-rounded presentation, you have to start with a holistic mentality. Take everything into consideration. What limitations does the location present? How does that change how you are going to be talking about the topic? If you are presenting early in the morning, then you might have to bring a little extra pep to your delivery to make sure your audience is focused and ready. When you have considered the variables, we can move on to how you are going to organize your speech.

2. Structure

It may seem like a great opportunity for you to take everything you have learned and just chuck it into your presentation without using a prescribed structure or format. This may not be very productive. As you know by now, presenting is not only about the content. It also involves strategically organizing a speech in the most pleasing and understandable way possible. There is a reason the Greeks didn't stuff their speeches with information and the possibility that you have found a new, successful way of presenting in the thousands of years between us and the Greeks is a little far-fetched. Yes, aspects can be tweaked and changed and nothing is ever truly perfect, but the reason we continue to use the structures of the Greeks and Romans is because they work. Audiences respond well to these elements and they make public speaking easier for presenters.

The Romans combined arrangement and style into what we today know as format and structure. These concepts deal with arranging what you are going to say and the words you are going to use in a logical and pleasing way. Based on this structure, the aim is to arrange the presentation into three sections; mainly, the introduction, body, and conclusion. Humans have a habit of thinking in linear terms, from start to finish, from point A to point B. Therefore, using this structure will not only make sense to the audience, but will allow you to structure your presentation logically.

Figuring out how you are going to deliver your speech begins with what kind of speech you have to give. Are you giving an informative speech in which you have to communicate a specific idea to the audience? Perhaps you are giving a persuasive speech and you have to convince the audience about your idea. You might also be giving a demonstrative speech where you have to show your audience how something works. The structure for these will be the same. However, the way you present them and the language you use will be different. This section will explain the basic structure used to organize a speech while providing tips and tricks for organizing a persuasive, informative, or demonstrative speech.

The Toastmasters (2017), an international nonprofit educational organization that specializes in public speaking, believe that a good starting structure involves telling the audience what you are going to talk about, talking about it, and then telling them what you have spoken about. This easy three-point structure is a great place to start when you are feeling lost. In case you feel that this three-point structure may be too simple, I will remind you of the words of former Prime Minister of the United Kingdom, Winston Churchill, "If you have an important point to make, don't try to be subtle or clever. Use a pile driver. Hit the point once. Then come back and hit it again. Then hit it a third time—a tremendous whack!" The goal is to communicate effectively and using a simple structure to format your speech will give you an opportunity to do this.

- Introduction

As with most things in life, we have to start at the beginning, which in this case, is the introduction. As the Toastmasters suggest, you have to tell your audience what you are going to be discussing. The best thing you can do is to open with a striking thought or idea. Don't introduce yourself first or start getting into technicalities. Step onto the stage and grab your audience's attention. Your introduction should not make up more than ten percent of your speech. This is because the introduction does not actually provide the information you want to communicate, but it merely informs the audience about your presentation. The bulk of the speech should be in the body.

Using the example of climbing, you might not want to start with an unenthusiastic, "Hi, my name is Alex and today I'm going to talk to you about climbing." You will have already lost the audience and trying to get their attention back would be incredibly challenging. Instead, start with a full and bright,

> "Did you know that Alex Honnold was the first person to scale El Capitan without any safety gear?" (Feel free to point to a picture of the mountain if you are using technology to aid your presentation.) "Hi, my name is Alex. I am a personal trainer, and today I am going to be telling you a bit about free soloing. I am going to show you how to prepare for an expedition, what the dos and don'ts of free soloing are, as well as where you can find the best climbing spots."

As you can see, your introduction has fulfilled three outcomes. Firstly, you have grabbed the audience's attention. Secondly, you have introduced yourself and told the audience why you are here and why they should trust you and lastly, you have prepared them for the rest of the presentation by outlining what you will be discussing.

A good introduction is clear, concise, and informative. If your introduction is confusing and misleading, then your audience will struggle to connect with what you are saying. Starting strongly will allow you to guide your audience to the next section of your presentation, which is the body.

- Body

This is where the bulk of your information will be discussed. The optimal structure for a ten-minute speech involves three main points, three explanations, and three transitions. Your body will look something like this:

- Main point #1
  - Explanation
    - Transition
- Main Point #2
  - Explanation
    - Transition
- Main Point #3
  - Explanation
    - Transition

As highlighted in your introductory paragraph, your first point will be how to prepare for a climbing exhibition. Your speech may sound like this:

> "So, let's get started. Firstly, I am going to show you what you need to do to prepare for a safe and fun-filled climbing trip. Many people think you only have to bring snacks and water, but climbing can be a grueling and dangerous sport. You need to make sure you have all of the necessary

climbing equipment and safety harnesses." (At this point, you could elucidate what this gear might be and how much would be required for a safe climb. After you have elaborated further, you can begin to transition to the next point.) You can transition by saying, "Climbing is supposed to be fun, and if you know your safety is a priority, then nothing can hold you back. While you are having fun and being safe, it is important to take note of some important dos and don'ts of climbing."

Remember, if you only have ten minutes, you don't want to overwhelm the audience with facts, tips and tricks, and advice. You need to decide what the most important points are and communicate them effectively, instead of information-dumping.

- Conclusion

Conclusions may seem futile at times. You've said what you wanted to, so why include a closing paragraph? On the contrary, a conclusion can help your audience to draw everything you said together and leave with a comprehensive understanding of the topic you addressed. Conclusions are a time for the audience to make sense of everything you said in the introduction and main body. They should include a quick summary of the presentation (only one sentence), a call to action, and then you can thank the audience and walk off the stage. Just like how you made a punchy entrance, making a gracious exit will allow your audience to bask in the information you supplied.

3. Call to action

Usually appearing at the end of the presentation, this is the perfect time to motivate your audience. Whether you are giving a motivational, informative, descriptive, or persuasive presentation, giving your audience something to do will make them feel valued, inspired, and will also help your cause. A call to action can be something along the lines of:

- Donating
- Calling a business
- Sending an application
- Trying something new
- Helping someone
- Finding out more

Depending on your topic and what kind of presentation you are giving, your call to action will be something that benefits you and your cause. A call to action is a powerful way to grab your audience's attention one last time.

What to Avoid

1. Winging it

This is probably the worst thing you could do when public speaking, especially if you are anxious and lack the confidence to follow through. Sure, some people are great at winging it. They can come up with interesting topics on the spot and present in an understandable and streamlined manner. However, for the vast majority of us, that is simply not the case. Preparing is one of the most important steps in your public speaking journey. If you have an idea of what you want to say and how you are going to say it, you will be able to understand your abilities and begin to feel confident in them. Remember what I said about anxiety? The more you know, the less you have to worry about.

2. Not being aware of the context

The next chapter will deal specifically with delivering speeches at work, school, and social events; however, the importance of context should not be lost on us. The context tells us whether we need to be formal or informal, and whether we can include stories or if we should stick to data representation. What about tone? Can you make a few jokes or would the audience perhaps question your credibility if you did? When you prepare for your presentation, it is important to keep in mind who your audience is, what you are presenting, and what is expected of you. If you have this information, preparing for your speech will be quick and easy. It will also allow you to prepare an appropriate and effective speech.

3. Too much information

This is especially applicable to professional and work-related presentations. Often, we want to get as much information into our speeches as possible. This is not always the best way to present. Consider, for instance, how you respond to these two sentences:

- 95 percent of people find that preparing 70 percent of their speeches will lead to an 80 percent chance of success when public speaking.
- The majority of people find that preparing for presentations leads to a higher success rate.

The first sentence requires the audience to think a lot more when actually all you want to do is give them one main piece of information. If your presentation is stuffed with data, then the audience will find it difficult to concentrate and your speech will be ineffective. When you are making your outline, you can include these percentages and numbers, but make sure that you are addressing the point when you give your presentation.

4. Not planning for pauses

Sometimes planning for speeches in our heads and on paper does not account for expression, tone, emotion, or pauses. We don't really want to deliver our speech as though we are reading it off of a prompter or cue cards. Even the Romans knew that giving a speech is about way more than just what you have to say. It's about how you say it. The art of the pause can be quite tricky because you have to plan for it. Sometimes, a joke won't stick and your pause might feel forced and awkward. Other times, you may get the audience all riled up, but deny them the opportunity to bask in the moment. Either way, making sure you have enough pauses in the right places will ensure that both you and your audience are comfortable. If you are unsure about where to put them, try reading your speech aloud, read it to a close friend, or record yourself and decide where you think a pause would be best suited.

5. This is not a roast

This applies to giving speeches in an informal context, unless it really is a roast, then, by all means, have at it. However, often we mistake meanness for comedy. This is rarely the case. As I said, unless it is an actual roast, don't be unkind to the people around you. This is definitely not the way to get the audience on your side. It will most likely leave you feeling ashamed and embarrassed and leave your audience a little upset. Be gracious, kind, and supportive and your audience will reward you.

6. Complicating your message

Similarly to reducing the amount of data in your presentation, delivering an uncomplicated and simple speech can lead to a successful outcome. Remember, public speaking is about communicating effectively. If you are not getting to the point, or are decorating your speech with superfluous information, your audience won't know where to look. Strip your speech down to the bare necessities and lock in exactly what you want to say before you add any additional information. Sometimes, this information can be extremely helpful to the audience; however, it must support the main intention and not detract from it.

7. Don't be boring

Have you ever arrived at work to find that, first thing in the morning, you have to listen to a presentation? Oh, how you dread those few minutes as you sip on your cup of coffee. This could go one of two ways. Either your morning takes a turn for the better and you are perked up and inspired by the presentation or you find yourself jerking awake to the sound of your colleagues giving a slow and unenthusiastic clap as the presentation comes to an end. Which one would you rather experience? Sure, the latter might be great if you have been struggling to sleep, but at the end of the day, we all want to walk away from a presentation feeling revitalized, renewed, and excited. This is what you have to give your audience. Use props, be excited and confident, find different and engaging ways of expressing yourself, and tell stories. There are so many tools, tips, and tricks for you to utilize that you really don't have any excuses for delivering a boring presentation. You know how you want to feel, so make it happen for your audience.

8. Do not open with a definition

While it can be useful to open with an explanation of sorts, if you are going to give a speech at a wedding, do not start with the Oxford Dictionary definition of *love*. This is outdated and dry and will leave your audience cringing. Perhaps if you are giving a speech on stock analysis, a definition might be useful, but in any other situation, it is just plain cheesy. And not the good kind either.

9. Repetition

It might seem necessary to repeat yourself at times, and sometimes it is valid and helpful for the audience if they make those connections for you. However, most of the time, the audience will understand what you are referring to and the repeated words will only take up valuable time and concentration. Your audience can be very fragile and even the slightest hint of mono-tonality and repetition can send their minds daydreaming. If you have to reiterate a point, try using synonyms or phrasing the sentence differently. Variety is key when attempting to maintain the audience's attention. However, repetition can also be used to your advantage. If you are trying to emphasize or build up to a point, repetition can excite the audience. It might sound something like this:

> "Together, we can make a change. Together, we can fight the fight. And together, we will bask in the glory of our victory."

In this case, repetition works. But don't repeat points you have already made because this can come off as clumsy and unprofessional.

Tips for Writing a Stellar Speech

- Open with a quote

By opening with a quote, you can create some intrigue around your topic. You can draw your audience in immediately and leave them excited about what is to come. The audience probably does not know what you will be speaking about and keeping them on their toes can benefit you greatly. Quotes are a great way to introduce the topic, call the audience to action, and motivate the audience all in one, before you have even introduced yourself. Just make sure the quote you use applies to the topic. If you don't, it can be confusing for everyone and your credibility can be put into question. Try to quote an industry professional and keep it relevant. There's no point in quoting Ariana Grande when you are giving a speech on strategic investing.

- Make the call to action reachable

You have to keep in mind who your audience is. If you are pitching to wealthy investors, then your call to action should not be *go check out our website*. You know that they are able to contribute more meaningfully to your purpose and you can therefore ask them for expertise, donations, and facilities. However, you also do not want to make your audience feel inadequate and unconfident by giving them too large a call to action. Be sensitive to your audience and their needs. If you are giving a presentation at work, motivate your colleagues to improve their performance or reach higher output targets. You should not be motivating them to make donations to the marketing department. Remember the context, listen to the audience, and make them feel inspired.

- Research

I cannot stress how important this is to the success of your presentation. If you are going to give an accurate, honest, and helpful presentation, then you have to understand the topic you are discussing. It is your duty as the presenter to provide the correct information to your audience. If you do not, this could have far-reaching implications, not only for your presentation, but for your career. You could nullify your credibility as a reliable source.

- Be aware of transitions

You have outlined the three main parts of your presentation and you are so excited to go through them that you rush through each point, sprint to the conclusion, and pant your way off the stage. Transitions are important because they guide the audience. Unlike the written word, we cannot identify paragraphs, pauses, or exclamations without a little help from the way we speak. Therefore, you have to guide the audience to the next paragraph and point. Be careful about making these transitions too abrupt. Try to incorporate them naturally into the presentation by summarizing the first point and commenting on its relation to the next point. Abrupt changes can disorientate the audience and reduce their ability to focus for the duration of the speech.

- Play on human emotion

The Greeks referred to this as *Pathos*. This is the emotional side of public speaking. *Pathos* was, and still is, widely used in the theatre. Actors would be instructed to play on the emotions of pity and fear. Fear can be a powerful emotion to play on because it makes us act in desperation. I'm not saying your speeches have to induce fear; however, adding a little stress and excitement to your speech may benefit you.

- Include stories

Public Speaking Coach and Founder of BostonSpeaks (a public speaking training organization), Kit Pang (2020), uses storytelling to play on the emotions of his audience. Pang explains that when you listen to stories, your brain produces dopamine, cortisol, and oxytocin. As we know, dopamine and oxytocin are the chemicals that make us feel good, excited, and happy, but what is cortisol (the stress hormone) doing there? Well, this is where the idea of stress and fear come into play. If the audience is sitting at the edge of their seat because of the story you are telling them, then you have their attention. By bringing a little bit of stress into your presentation, like telling a story that has a time limit or an element of danger, the audience will perk up and listen to you.

Not only that, Pang says that stories are 22 times more memorable to the human brain than any other manner of relaying information. Humans communicate through stories, anecdotes, expressions, and emotions, so why not utilize those aspects to your advantage? Of course, stories are not relevant to all presentations, so you probably don't want to tell your colleagues about that time you mixed salt in your chocolate cake instead of sugar because that has nothing to do with long-term investing. However, having stories in your arsenal can push you that little step further to help you win the audience over.

Organizing your speech can feel intimidating and impossible at times, but taking it step-by-step will allow you to focus on what your true goal is, and that is to communicate effectively. Make sure you are saying what you need to say and getting your message across in a digestible and exciting way.

Chapter 6:

How to Prepare Speeches for Different Settings

As I have mentioned in the preceding chapters, context is extremely important to your public speaking success. You may have prepared the most amazing presentation about your summer vacation, but if you are presenting it at a board meeting, you could fail monumentally. This chapter is going to show you how to effectively prepare a speech for work, school, or a social event. For each context, you will be provided with an outline for your audience, how to prepare your speech, how to deliver your speech, and what tips and tricks you can use to enhance your presentation. Keeping your context in mind is crucial to effective communication, but don't worry! At the end of this chapter, you will be equipped for any situation.

In the Workplace

You might feel a lot of pressure when presenting at work. You are surrounded by peers and superiors, you have to triple check all of your data, and you have to make sure people are informed and even impressed by your speech. Effective communication is always necessary, but in the workplace, it could make or break your career. Unless you have a relaxed work environment where you sit on bean bags and have Frappuccinos on tap at the company coffee shop, then chances are that your speech is going to require some formality and professionalism. However, this does not mean that it has to be boring and mundane. Sure, the content may be full of numbers, percentages, and strategies, but there are ways to make this information digestible. But first, who are you presenting to?

- Audience

Is this a routine presentation based on company incentives and output? In this case, the audience will most likely consist of your peers and subordinates. This is the perfect chance to instill some motivation and to add a meaningful call to action at the end of your presentation. This also means that, on one hand, you can be a bit more relaxed because you are in charge. On the other hand, you have a responsibility to your peers and subordinates to guide them and set an example for them to follow.

What if you have to present to your colleagues and superiors? This situation can definitely cause more stress because you are trying to impress them. While a call to action is still important, it may be more significant to show them how you will provide a call to action to your team. In that way, they can monitor your progress and see that you are dedicated and motivated.

As you have probably been to a few work presentations in your time, you know that feeling bored is a personal battle. On one hand, it's just so boring. But on the other hand, you have to listen to what is being presented because it could impact your productivity and that of the company your work for. So, don't be that person; the one who relays tons of data to their staff in the hopes that they retain at least a third of it. While you may not be dramatically inclined, public speaking involves a bit of theatre and the three most important elements in a play are the actors, the message, and the audience. These three elements are also essential to public speaking in any and every context. You don't have to put on a show at work, but you do have to be interesting and entertaining for your audience.

Your audience is one that requires specific information. Therefore, you have to be concise and output-driven. They don't want to sit there and hear about what you did last week or that you just got engaged. They want facts, statistics, strategies, and direction. Giving them what they want and need will allow you to prepare and deliver your speech in a pleasing and constructive manner.

- Preparation

Preparing and planning your speech might look a little different from the format I provided in the previous chapter. Your speech will most likely be informative, but could also be motivational, demonstrative, and persuasive. Therefore, you have to figure out how you need to prepare. An informative speech is quite straightforward to format. You will most likely have to relay information about your team's work and progress. You may also have to present the future strategies of the business and what this will mean for the employees.

Informative presentations might look something like this:

> "Today we are going to discuss the financial year of [insert company name]. We have excelled in some areas and declined in others. I will talk about our performance, and provide strategies for the next financial year. Firstly, we have far exceeded our output expectations and have experienced a growth of three percent. This is largely due to our dedication as a team, open communication lines, and the introduction of new quantifying programs that have decreased our processing times. To maintain this level of growth, we will need to focus on the following areas..."

You would then move on to the next few points and your conclusion. As you can see, the language used is clear, concise, and contextually relevant. Your audience will learn that the business is doing well and they will also know why this is so. They will come to find out where they can improve and how they can implement these strategies in the future. Preparing a persuasive speech will most likely be targeted towards your superiors or clients. This presentation could take the shape of a pitch and might sound like this:

> "I am here today to show how we can improve our output margin. Our current systems are outdated and complicated. I have identified a more efficient data capturing system which I will be discussing,

along with how we can practically implement these systems into the company's ecosystem."

Again, the language is to the point and informative. You might notice that it is a little punchier than the example of the informative speech. This is because persuasion requires a little more tact and enthusiasm. You are trying to convince people why you are right, or why your product is right for them. Show them the benefits and make sure you have a strategy in place. Raising issues can be easier than finding appropriate solutions. Ensure that you have included useful solutions in your presentation.

Motivational speeches may not be as common because there should always be an element of motivation in the informative or persuasive speeches you give at work. Alternatively, demonstrative presentations are useful when you have to inform people of a new technique or filing system that is being implemented at work. The presentations will most likely be formatted in a similar way to the informative presentation; however, instead of including three main points, the body may discuss:

1. What is the new system?
2. What are the steps that need to be followed?
3. Why will this help the company and improve productivity?

Deciding what format your speech should take will allow you to get into what you are actually going to be presenting. How you present this will be discussed next regarding the delivery of a speech.

- Delivery

Because presentations at work are more formal, the delivery of your speech needs to reflect a certain level of professionalism. In this case, eye contact, body language, and posture are very important in creating an authoritative aura. Think about when you were a child, and there was a parent that you listened to no matter what. Even if they just raised an eyebrow at you, you knew there was trouble. However, when the day came where that parent was out doing something and you were stuck with the other one, try as they might, shout and scream, and lose control, you just would not listen to them. This is because you did not perceive them as having authority. Similarly, in the workplace, if you want people to listen, you have to have an air of confidence, knowledgeability, and assertiveness. Credibility is a particularly necessary aspect of speaking in the workplace because people must trust you to be inclined to listen to you. They need to trust that what you are saying is the truth, so that they can be productive employees.

Try to utilize colorful (not too colorful though, because this can be distracting and childlike) charts, graphs, and diagrams. If you are dealing with a lot of data, then showing something on a pie chart is a great way of making something quite complicated, easy to understand. Ask yourself what sounds better:

1. First-time consumers make up 53 percent of our total yearly revenue while 21 percent of this comes

from repeat consumers and 26 percent from wholesalers.
2. Alternatively, you can use a pie chart consisting of three colors, each representing one of the factors contributing to the total yearly revenue.

Instead of having to picture the chart for yourself and do the calculations, the pie chart does the thinking for the audience which allows them to focus on the rest of your presentation. It's not about getting as much information into your presentation as you possibly can, it's about using your presentation time effectively and time-consciously. Too many colors or numbers can distract the audience and detract from the message of your presentation.

- Tips and tricks
    - Online presentations

Because we live in a digital age, we don't necessarily need to attend every meeting in person. We also live in an interconnected world which means meeting in person is not always a possibility. When presenting online, it is important to firstly, wear your entire work outfit. Yes, I see you with your pajama bottoms on! If you are doing this, your headspace may be in two contradicting places. On one hand, you're in work mode and on the other, you are slouched on the couch watching television and eating cereal. I doubt you would show up to a presentation like that in your office, so don't do it over a video call, even if no one can see you.

You may not be able to move around as much as you would in person, so make sure you keep your body language interesting with hand gestures and facial expressions. Also, run through your slides before you present. I am sure you have been on a conference call where the slides are all mixed up, the presenter is confused, you are confused, and no one remembers the last thing that was said. Check that your slides are streamlined and in place.

People have more distractions at home, so it can be easier for them to lose focus on a video call. Try to add motion and sound clips to your slides to reel the audience back in and attract their interest. And just because it's online and people are at home, does not mean that you can talk for forty minutes unless absolutely necessary. Keep it concise, keep it clear, and make sure people walk away revitalized and not wondering what the point of the meeting was.

- Don't add fluff

Which brings us to this point... don't add too much fluff. What do I mean by fluff? I mean all of the unnecessary information that might sound good or look nice, but does not add any value to your presentation. Just like your language, you want to keep it clear and crisp, with no distractions or pretense. You do not need to tell a five-minute story about how you used a filing system at your previous job and how Bob filed everything backwards. Or how every time you try to color code something, you mix up green and blue because you're semi-colorblind. These tidbits don't add any value for the audience, and quite the opposite, they are a distraction. People will leave wondering whether the presentation was about the filing system or your old work colleague, Bob. It might be fun and interesting to include something like this when you are giving a speech at a social event, but the workplace is not the setting for cute anecdotes. Stick to the script and get to the point. You might think that this would deflate your sense of creativity, but there is much room for expression within the boundaries of professionalism. As long as you make sure your point and the information don't get lost in creativity, your presentation will be effective and successful.

- Don't make it too simple

I know, I just told you to keep it clear and simple, but there is such a thing as making your presentation too simple. You want to explain your main points and get the message across and if you are just reading bullet-point lists, then your audience may not fully understand what you are getting at. The same applies with making slides for a presentation. Don't just put on a single sentence verbatim what you are going to say to the audience. Make sure the slides and elements you use add value and information and don't just reiterate and repeat what you have already shown.

- Dealing with tough bosses and pressure

It can be difficult to deal with negativity or constructive criticism. Hard-to-please bosses can leave us feeling inferior and incapable. Unfortunately, we can't please everyone. If you are unsure about something, ask. Work on precedence, look at what has been done before, and take note of how you can impress your superiors. At the end of the day, all you can do is make sure you have done the job and done it well; the rest is in their hands. Remember that failure is a learning opportunity.

Similarly to how you have to change your perception of failure, changing your view of pressure can allow you to actualize your potential. Use the pressure to drive yourself forward instead of being intimidated. Pressure and stress can be crippling, especially when work consumes our daily lives. While work is important, it is not everything. Do what is necessary, but also give yourself space and time to live your life. Your presentations will be better for it and you will find that confidence comes far more easily. You aren't a diamond, so millions of years of stress are not going to shape you into an expensive rock. On the contrary, you could just end up as a piece of coal. Let the pressure inspire you.

At School

Giving a speech at school or for college can be considerably less formal; however, there are situations in which formality is pertinent. School presentations can vary from in-class speeches to proposing your thesis to lecturers and your peers. Sometimes, it can also mean hosting a guest lecture. Giving presentations at university signifies that you will have to give speeches about things you don't really know much about (if you are in an undergraduate program). This is where presenting at school can be different from presenting at work. At work, you are the expert and a professional, but at school, you have to follow a set of guidelines set up by your lecturer and what is required from the course. Staying within these boundaries can be difficult and so can speaking about something that you don't know much about. Luckily, I am here to provide you with some guidance on how to successfully prepare and deliver a presentation at school, university, or college.

- Audience

First, we have to figure out who will be attending your presentation. Is this a class presentation that does not count towards your grades? Perhaps you can adopt a more informal approach to the tone and content of the presentation. While it might seem like giving a speech in an informal setting is easier, it can still be quite nerve-wracking. It is okay to feel a fair amount of pressure, so just remember to be confident and to breathe. It is likely that this kind of presentation will be informative or demonstrative. You will either be telling the class about something or showing them how something works. Try to keep it as basic as possible as you may not be the only person giving a presentation. Your audience might already be exhausted from all the information they have taken in during the lesson. Bombarding them with more terms and concepts would be detrimental to your presentation. As with every presentation, do the work for your audience, let them sit back, relax, and learn from you.

Is the presentation going to be evaluated? The pressure of getting a good grade can impact how you view the presentation. This speech may have to take on a more formal and professional tone. In this case, the audience will be more attentive, but again, because you might be one of several students giving a presentation, it is crucial to keep it simple. Make sure you explain all of the concepts to the audience and add a short definition on your slides every once in a while. Sometimes school and university topics can be complex and making them digestible and understandable can take a lot of effort and explaining. Use analogies to make these concepts easier to understand.

Do you have to present your dissertation to lecturers and peers? This can be intimidating because the success of your dissertation also depends on how well you can explain it. If you complicate it too much, your lecturers may view your dissertation as far-reaching and unattainable. If you make it too simple, they may think you have not put enough effort into your research. Finding a balanced middle ground is essential for effectively communicating your thesis statement. Try to break down a few terms and concepts, but remember that you are presenting to lecturers, and people who understand the material, so give them some credit. Use the necessary target vocabulary and show them that you have a deep and holistic understanding of the terms.

- Preparation

Preparing for a formally-graded presentation involves far more than good content. You will most likely be graded on your performance, voice, content, and your ability to interact with the audience. For the rest of these, you will find strategies throughout the book; however, in terms of formatting the content of your presentation, you can learn that right here. Using the same three-point structure for your school presentation is an easy way to guarantee great results. It is likely to be an informative presentation which might be structured like this:

> "Did you know the Ancient Egyptians were the first people to perform a Cesarean section on a pregnant woman? Today, I am going to tell you about the medical feats of the Egyptians and how these experiments, procedures, and inventions have influenced modern medicine."

This example is effective because it starts with a rhetorical question and a fact that most people are unlikely to know. You will have peaked the audience's attention to gain their interest in the topic. Playing on the audience's curiosity can help you to deliver a successful speech. It is also simple and to the point, making it easy to follow.

What if you have to present as part of a group? How do you stand out in a group presentation and make sure the rest of your team is also successful? Group work can be a drag or it can be an enlightening experience that allows everyone to learn ten times more than they thought they would. It is all about how you view it. Perhaps in the past, you might not have enjoyed group work because it is basically public speaking, just in front of a small audience. However, with your newfound voice and confidence, group work might become your favorite thing to do. Talking to people is a good way to learn.

Everyone has their own unique way of seeing the world and sharing these views can give you a more consolidated and multi-faceted view of the world. If you enter into the group with a positive mindset and energy, you will soon be able to motivate and inspire your team. See it as a practice round for your actual presentation.

There are many ways you could go about doing a group presentation. You could split the presentation into several sections and give each person a section to research and present. This is risky because it means your presentation will lack consistency and continuity. You also won't know how the other people in your group went about researching, so there could be inconsistencies in credibility which bring your beautifully researched work into question.

You might try completing the presentation together which would solve the inconsistency issue, but might bring up some conflict. Everyone has a different way of doing their work. At the end of the day, a combination of these two methods will allow for a successful and well-rounded presentation. Do the research together, and make an outline for each section you want to address. When each section has been thoroughly researched, each person can take a section home and write it how they are comfortable saying it. When everyone has compiled their sections, a group edit can be done to fact-check, ensure consistency, and polish any rough spots.

Since these may be your first encounters with public speaking at a higher level, you may make use of cue cards. These can be problematic, especially if you are anxious at the thought of speaking in front of an audience. The cue cards could become a crutch and you could end up reading them instead of connecting with your audience. In this case, it is important not to write your entire presentation out, but only use a few keywords for each section to remind yourself what you have to speak about. Cue cards can be effective to get you out of your shell to make you feel more confident in your abilities, but just like the training wheels on a bicycle, they have to come off eventually.

You also have to consciously consider the guidelines set up by your teacher and course. Similarly to how context is important to giving a successful presentation, so is staying on topic. If you are being graded on your knowledge and ability to speak about a specific topic, then you must adhere to that topic. You must not get side-tracked and start talking about the medical discoveries of the Aztecs when you are being graded on your knowledge of the Ancient Egyptians. Remember to research relevant information. Sure, the Aztecs also might have made revolutionary medical discoveries, but that's not the point. If you want to get the grades, stick to the outline.

- Delivery

Confidence is always going to be important when delivering a speech whether it is at work, school or at a social event. Ensure you have that confidence on lock. In terms of delivering a presentation at school, you have a lot more room to play with tone variation and body language than you do at work presentations. So, switch up your tone, tell a joke or two, and make sure the audience is entertained. The majority of your audience will be young students. Their attention spans are short and they are able to focus on many things at once. You have to give them a reason to focus their energy on you. If your presentation is informative, try adding a playful tone to it, and tell a fun story or an interesting fact to keep them listening and on their toes.

Conversely, when presenting your thesis statement to your lecturers and superiors, try to maintain a formal and knowledgeable tone. Anecdotes are useful, but jokes might be perceived as misplaced in this case. Dress professionally and show them that you are serious. I will give you tips on dressing for the part in the upcoming chapters, but for now, you just need to know that presenting yourself in a professional manner will force your audience to take you seriously and to not question your credibility.

- Tips and tricks
  - Online presentations

Similarly to giving work presentations online, check that your slides are in order and you are appropriately dressed. Try to add more diagrams and information onto your slides because sometimes you may run into technical difficulties with your microphone and the sound might be temperamental. Make sure that even if the audience cannot hear you, they can understand you through your slides. Even though you are at home and able to read your entire speech off the computer without losing engagement with your audience, I would still advise you to use keywords. This will train your brain to memorize better and will give you the skill of adapting to your presentation situations. If you are in front of an audience one day, it would be nice to know that you can execute the presentation even if you did forget something or you got distracted. Thinking on your feet can save you and also give the speech a natural, conversational tone, instead of a forced reading voice.

- Tell stories

Storytelling might not have a place at work, but it can be extremely effective in less formal situations like at school or university. Your peers are more likely to be entertained and they will walk away with a better understanding of the topic at hand. When you do tell these stories, just remember to link them to what you are discussing in your presentation. You might have a superb story about fishing in Alaska, but this does not have anything to do with your presentation on Ancient Egypt. Guide the audience. Don't make them work for it.

- Don't be afraid to ask for help

Schools and universities are places for learning which means that you will be challenged in ways that you have never been before. It is okay to ask your lecturers for help and guidance. The confidence you learned in the previous chapters will help you to find the assertiveness necessary to talk to your superiors and pick their brains. If they are unable to help you, you can rely on an entire university filled with educated and capable people. Public speaking is about more than just speaking in front of an audience; it is about speaking to people in a calm, confident, and effective manner.

- Clarify complicated concepts

Unlike giving a presentation at work where everyone is aware of the jargon, school presentations require a little more explanation. Teachers will often use these presentations to educate and inform the rest of the class on a topic, which means that no one will initially know what you are talking about. Therefore, it is important to clarify and explain all terms that you didn't know when you started researching your topic. Try to provide labeled and simple diagrams and pictures to make it easier to grasp and more fun to learn.

At a Social Event

Contrastingly to giving a presentation at work or school, speeches at social events are far more forgiving. You probably don't have to wear a blazer and tie, you don't have to do much research, and you can incorporate a joke or two. However, this does not mean that you can just get up in front of your audience and wing it. You still have to put some thought into the preparation of your presentation and be conscious of how you deliver it. You might be able to tell a joke or two, but these jokes have to be appropriate and context-specific. You also have to be conscious of your audience. Are they conservative, liberal, old-fashioned, or young? What do they find funny and what would they classify as inappropriate?

- Audience

Your audience can make or break you and paying careful attention to their wants and needs at a social gathering can help you considerably. Is the audience comfortable and enthusiastic? You may want to use this to spur them on and play on their enthusasm. Mainly, the audience will depend on the kind of gathering you are having. If it is a small gathering of friends and family, then your demeanor can be more casual and relaxed as opposed to professional and knowledgeable. In the case of public speaking at social events, these presentations can be congratulatory, informative, introductory or acceptance speeches. You might get a persuasive one every now and then, if you have to convince your friends and family to do something or change something. Maybe you are convincing them to quit consuming sugar, in which case you will need a very compelling argument. However, most of the time you will just need to tell them something. You can use a friendly tone and remember to be yourself. These people know you well and speaking to them will come naturally to you.

But what if you have to speak at a big event like a wedding or a funeral? Sure, you might be surrounded by family, but you will also be surrounded by people you don't know (unless it's your wedding, of course). In this case, do some research about who makes up the audience. You don't want to make a joke loaded with sexual innuendo if most of the audience will be there with their children. Make sure that your speech is kind. Remember, this isn't a roast and you don't want to ruin someone's special day by trying to be funny. Alternatively, at a funeral, you probably don't want to make any jokes. However, this is dependent, once again, on the audience. Perhaps they view funerals as somber events that should be sad and sorrowful, in which case you should maintain a serious tone. However, if your audience is of the opinion that life is to be celebrated, then small stories and anecdotes about the deceased's life can help bring joy to the audience. Giving speeches at social events is all about the audience.

What if you have to give a speech at a social event for work? In this case, you would have to maintain a semblance of professionalism, but also make sure you are charming and entertaining. Is the event a fundraiser, an end of year function, or a gala? Either way, the audience expects you to be on your best behavior because you will be representing your company. Make sure you understand your audience and what they might like or dislike and prepare your speech with this information in mind.

- Preparation

Preparing for a small gathering is not grueling nor does it require the same format that we have been using up to this point. You might only have one or two things to say, as opposed to laying out a three-point plan with explanations and transitions. A speech for your family and friends might look like this:

> "Hello everyone. I have gathered you here today because I want to inform you that I am moving to

Canada in three months. I got a job in Vancouver and wanted to share the great news with you all."

These kinds of speeches are short and to the point, and most of the information will come afterwards when they begin to ask you questions. You won't need to prepare cue cards or slides of any sort because you just want to tell them one thing. If you show them a bunch of slides of Canada and start explaining what your new job will be in great detail, they might get confused and not understand your intention. Remember, even though the audience is made up of your friends and family, you still have to communicate effectively.

So, how do you prepare a speech for a larger social event like a wedding or funeral? This kind of speech has to be a bit more thought out. If you are speaking at a wedding, then you will probably be congratulating the happy couple. Because these speeches can be more informal, you don't have to start with an outline of what you are going to say because that would be formal and weird. Instead, you can introduce yourself as the father of the bride, mother of the groom, or best man/woman. Whoever you are, not everyone will know you and it is a good piece of context for the audience to have. The rest of the speech may start with a story:

> "Three years ago, on the coldest Christmas Day we had in ten years, we were introduced to our daughter's partner. Since then, we have seen her grow and thrive with [insert partner's name] and we could not be happier to share this day with them. We are thrilled to officially have you in our

> family and we can't wait to see how you two continue to love and support each other."

The speech is kind, thoughtful, and pays tribute to the occasion. You could add another story and introduce other characters, but speeches at social events should generally be kept short and sweet. If you do want to give a longer speech, then use the same three-point format I have outlined previously. However, the transitions will be far smoother and the format will not be as clear cut as "point, explanation, transition." The format can be used to guide your speech and everything you would like to include, but should remain conversational and natural.

If you are speaking at a work function, then you will have to set out a more in-depth outline. If you are required to give an introductory speech, then you will have to welcome the audience and thank them for their attendance and support. You will then have to shed light on the occasion and why their attendance is necessary and valued. For example, if you have to give an introductory speech at a charity gala for endangered animals, you may start by saying:

> "Good evening and thank you for coming." You would then proceed to introduce the reason for the gala which is to raise funds for the Black Rhino. You can include more information here and perhaps start to introduce the three main points of discussion. Finally, you could end with: "We hope to shed light on the topic and raise enough money to make a meaningful change. Your contributions are encouraged and valued."

Similarly to presentations at work, you have clearly and concisely discussed the topic at hand. It may be useful to include why your company is hosting this gala and why the survival of the Black Rhino is significant to your company. Depending on the topic, a short story or anecdote can be a helpful way to motivate your audience and grab their attention.

- Delivery

For work functions, you want to maintain a conversational, but professional tone. The audience must feel at ease, but also that you are respectable, knowledgeable, and authoritative. Maintain a confident stance and posture throughout the speech and make sure you speak loudly and clearly. The odds are that the audience will be bigger than you are used to and you will have to project towards the back of the room. Keep in mind that because there are so many people there, some of them may be distracted; however, it is your job to grab their attention. This is a great time to start with a quote to inspire your audience. Remember, work functions will also require a significant and effective call to action. Play on their emotions. If you are telling them about endangered animals, then playing on their pity and sympathy could encourage larger donations. In addition, inciting a small amount of fear with regard to their potential extinction may also add an element of haste to your cause. Although, try not to overuse these techniques because people could start to feel too guilty and perhaps get annoyed and decide not to donate. So, while playing on the audience's emotions can be helpful, it can also be detrimental. Use this power wisely.

When delivering a speech at a large family gathering like a wedding, it is important to maintain a light-hearted tone. People don't want to be sad on this day and you probably shouldn't start talking about how you lost your job or how bad the economy is right now. Keep it light, keep it happy, and make sure you honor the cause. Once again, confidence is key, but try to maintain a less stiff and more causal confidence at these social events. People want to feel relaxed and at ease. They want to laugh and be merry. Unless you are giving a speech at a funeral, in which case you should be sensitive to the tone of the event.

- Tips and tricks
  - Don't drink too much

Sure, you may be at an event surrounded by your friends and family, and you want to dance a little and have some fun. While you are allowed to have fun, you do have responsibilities to consider. Give yourself a two-drink limit, at least until the speech is over, then you can do whatever you want. It is important to be in control and aware of yourself when you give a speech. Being someone who slurs and falls about during what is supposed to be a civilized and happy evening can ruin the event and your reputation. You also don't need to be inebriated to feel confident enough to face the crowd. The tools I have provided will be sufficient to get you up on that stage and speaking like a pro.

- Read the room

The audience is a key factor in how you will prepare and deliver your speech. At work and school, your audience will almost always demand true and reliable information relayed in an understandable and concise manner. At a social event, you have room for comedy, stories, emotion, and expression. Remember who you are talking to. If you know your aunt is conservative, don't make inappropriate jokes. Sure, you may succeed in being subversive, but that is not the goal here. Benjamin Franklin, one of the Founding Fathers of the United States, once said: "Remember not only to say the right thing in the right place, but far more difficult still, to leave unsaid the wrong thing at the tempting moment." Public speaking is just as much about what you don't say as it is about what you do say. Read the room and make sure everything you are communicating creates a healthy and open space for yourself and your audience.

Public speaking is an art and a challenging one at that. You have to be intuitive and adaptable while maintaining a level of clarity and transparency. To succeed and give a stellar presentation, you will have to be confident and keep context and audience in mind when you prepare your speech. After that, all you have to do is deliver it and believe it or not, that's going to feel like the easy part.

Chapter 7:

Tips on What to Do Before and After Your Speech

So far, we have discussed how to prepare yourself for your public speaking journey and how to prepare and deliver your presentation. But what do you do right before and immediately after your presentation? This can often be overlooked as you will be focused intently on what you are going to say and how you are going to say it. The moments just before your presentation can be a crucial preparation time for your brain and body to settle in before you step out in front of the audience. If you freak yourself out before you have to deliver your speech, then all of your planning and effort could be derailed and you might just turn into a blubbering mess—and no one wants to bear witness to that. It would be such a shame to do all of the introspection and confidence building just to have it fall apart in the last ten minutes.

What about after the speech? In terms of giving a presentation at work or school, you will most likely have to answer a few questions regarding your speech. This chapter will help you to prepare for the before and after, so that you won't be blindsided by questions and comments. On a more personal note, the time after your presentation is important for self-reflection. Where do you go from here? What are your next goals? To keep improving, you have to keep pushing and challenging yourself. You might brush this chapter off, thinking you know yourself and you know what triggers you before a presentation. Well, I'm here to tell you that the ten minutes before you go on can totally ruin your presentation, or make it the best speech you have ever given. Wouldn't you rather avoid the former?

Helpful Exercises to Prepare You for Your Speech

1. Set up a checklist

Checklists are a great way to make sure you are not forgetting anything. Sometimes we think we can remember everything, and we use little Post-its to remind ourselves to bring the cue cards, but having a comprehensive list of everything you need will allow you to focus on one thing at a time, while still getting everything done. Your checklist may look something like this:

- Cue cards
- Memory card/flash drive
- Bottle of water
- Reading glasses
- Business cards
- Laptop (and charger)
- HDMI cable

This might seem like a small and insignificant list, but forgetting just one of the elements might make giving your presentation impossible. If you don't remember your laptop or the HDMI cable, then you won't be able to present with the slides you made. Similarly, forgetting your glasses could make it difficult for you to read the cue cards and leaving your business cards behind could be detrimental to your post-presentation networking. I am not doubting your ability to remember a small list of items, but sometimes you will have a busy day, or your nerves may get the better of you. It is better to have a clear mind.

2. It's not just about the day of your presentation

You might think that presenting only requires mental preparation on the day of the presentation. Unfortunately, it is not that simple. You may have done everything right, made a checklist, and done your memory and breathing exercises, but if you had a bad night's rest, presenting the next day would be a challenge. It's kind of like going to the Olympics, and training for all those months, only to stop sleeping and start eating burgers a week before your event. You have to be dedicated and follow through up until the very moment your speech ends. Make sure you continue to practice your speech and fact check all of your information consistently.

You might think it unnecessary and mismatched, but because exercise is such a useful technique for overcoming fear and anxiety, it is also essential to exercise, eat healthily, and get enough sleep before your presentation. Don't just think, because you have found your voice and a little bit of confidence, that you don't have to maintain good health. Athletes train constantly and that's why they are so successful. So, don't back out on the last lap. Finish what you started and finish it well.

3. Get active

What does exercising have to do with public speaking? It might not directly have an impact on your public speaking, but making sure your body is happy, healthy, and flexible can help to improve your posture, which makes speaking through your diaphragm easier. Don't worry, I'm not saying that you have to become a fitness junkie to be a good public speaker (but if you are, it won't hurt). You don't have to fit into any specific body type or shape. However, having your abdominal, shoulder, and upper leg muscles activated can help you to stand taller, look more confident, and feel better about yourself.

Yes, that's right, exercising releases endorphins and serotonin which make us feel happy. Exercise can also be a valuable tool to boost your confidence (not just for looking confident) and your self-esteem. In terms of controlling your nerves ten minutes before you have to present, physical exercise can be a great way to expel some of that nervous energy. Maybe you don't need to do push-ups or sit-ups per se. You could dance, run in one spot, do an imaginary hop-scotch, or practice Tai Chi. This will allow you to stand in front of your audience energized and enthusiastic. You won't even remember that you were nervous. Although, try not to walk onto the stage panting. Just some light movement will be enough to get you going.

4. Have a glass of water

Basic, I know, but you won't believe how helpful drinking a simple glass of water can be. Specifically, if you are nervous, you might find your mouth starting to feel dry. It might feel like someone stuffed a few cotton balls into your mouth and you are struggling to breathe, let alone speak. A glass of water can be an easy fix ten minutes before your presentation, but what if this happens to you while you're on stage? You don't want to interrupt your own presentation halfway through to ask for a glass of water and then awkwardly gulp it down in front of your audience. They might feel uncomfortable at witnessing your nervousness and the interruption could cause them to lose focus. But, if your glass (or bottle) is already on stage, then you can use a pause to create some suspense, take a sip of your water and carry on as usual.

5. Don't read through it

You can do one of two things: pretend like nothing is happening, or visualize your success. Because you are already in a nervous state, you don't want those nerves to get your speech all mixed up. I can't tell you how many times I have seen it. A young, enthusiastic presenter, completely prepared and ready, pacing back and forth, flipping through cue cards, reciting every word of the speech in a jumbled, fast-forwarded sort of way. They take that manic energy onto the stage with them, start their speech and, oh dear, they have messed up the order of the cue cards...

They pause, look up all wide-eyed and pale. You see their left leg start to shake as their fingers paw through the rest of the cue cards to find the right one. The audience is confused and full of pity, and refocusing their attention would be nearly impossible at this point. The presenter freezes. They have forgotten everything.

If you have the urge to read through your speech, as I mentioned earlier, only read through the introduction and don't do so any later than ten minutes before your speech. Those ten minutes leading up to the presentation need to be spent being mindful and present or visualizing your success. Anything else will be futile and possibly detrimental.

    6. Get there early

I know I have been focusing on the ten minutes before the presentation; however, arriving early can also be helpful. Those ten minutes are usually filled with a lot of tension and nervous energy. Arriving early means you get to familiarize yourself with the setting, the audience, and the equipment. It leaves no room for surprises and less room for things to go wrong. Just like you have to practice and prepare for the presentation, you have to prepare yourself mentally for possible mishaps. This might be a good time to identify which three audience members you will focus on for the duration of your presentation. Otherwise, you may end up frantically looking around for friendly faces.

7. Get to know your audience

Odds are that when you were preparing your presentation you did some research on your audience; what they want, and what they like. This, however, is a different kind of preparation because it does not involve getting to know your audience as a whole, but individually. Meeting people before your presentation will distract you from the nerves of giving the presentation, but it will also allow you to humanize the audience. Instead of viewing the audience as a vague, undefined nimbus, you can see them as individuals who are excited to hear you present. In addition, this is a great way to push yourself out of your comfort zone. Meeting people can be scary, but if you are going to give a presentation in front of these people, then wouldn't you rather know them?

They will also appreciate your effort and perhaps give you more of their attention and focus throughout the presentation. Personalizing their experience could be the key to your success. Of course, try to make a good impression or otherwise this could leave a sour taste in their mouths. Come out with confidence, introduce yourself, get to know a little bit about them and thank them for coming. Similarly, if you are giving a presentation at work and you already know some of the people, make an effort to get to know them better. Public speaking is about creating human connections so that you can communicate effectively.

8. Be present

Remember when I said you have two options in the ten minutes before your speech? Well, this is one of them. Being present does not mean sitting there before your speech thinking of everything that can go wrong, rehearsing your speech, and worrying about whether you have something in your teeth. Being present is a type of meditation. This can be done through breathing and mindfulness. Use equal breaths and bring awareness to different parts of your body. This can take some practice. It is about being cognizant of your body and how it feels at that very moment. Start with something small like your toes or feet. Just pay attention to them, and nothing else. They may start to feel tingly and airy. This is good, as it means you are getting the hang of it. Then you can bring awareness to your wrists, ankles, from there your arms and legs, until you have gained awareness of your entire body while maintaining equal breathing. This whole process can take up to ten minutes and will act as the perfect transition point from pre-presentation jitters to in-presentation serenity.

9. Memory exercises

You might find that you struggle to remember your speech no matter how much you have practiced. This might be particularly true in the hours leading up to your presentation. As discussed, nerves can have that effect on people. So, before the day of your presentation, it is worthwhile to engage in some memory exercises. The first one is simple. Read your speech out loud. This jogs your memory as you can put yourself in a specific setting at a specific time. You might forget the next section of your speech, but suddenly remember how the sun was shining through your windows when you were reading aloud as practice. Without even trying, you will have been able to recall an important part of your speech as opposed to getting it. This method works because it places you in your reality. Another similar method that works specifically for your presentation can be to picture your house. It is a space that you know very well which makes it perfect for this exercise. As you go through your presentation, picture yourself saying different parts of your speech (in order) in different rooms of the house. But to make it even more effective, picture yourself saying them in strange positions, like while standing on the couch, or inside of the fireplace or under the table. Just like how you were able to remember the sun on that specific day, you will find it easier to remember the parts of your speech and the order in which to say them. The weirder it gets, the better.

Another effective method is to start playing mind games, like Scrabble, Sudoku, or crossword puzzles. There are loads of brain training apps readily available to you and they don't only help your memory, but they are also fun to do!

10. Warm-up exercises

Vocal exercises will not only help you to get rid of some of that nervous tension, they will also allow you to get your voice ready for the presentation. You don't want to walk out in front of the audience with a raspy or uneven voice. Appearing confident is also about how you sound and raspiness might make you sound unconfident and unsure, even though you might be feeling very confident and assured. Some vocal exercises you can use before your presentation and while practicing are:

- Stretch your checks out by blowing them up with air and move your jaw in a circular motion (clockwise and then-clockwise). While this is not a vocal exercise, it does loosen up the tension in your face which will allow you to appear relaxed and comfortable.
- Loosen your tongue by pushing air out of your mouth between your tongue and the roof of your mouth. This will create a "trr" sound which you should try to hold for an entire breath. Practice this a few times until the sound becomes smooth and can last for the duration of your breath.
- Sing a song that you like and that has great range (Bohemian Rhapsody by Queen will warm you up thoroughly). If you don't like doing strange mouth exercises and making weird noises, sing one of your favorite songs. The point is to get those vocal cords stretched, not to make yourself uncomfortable. When in doubt, sing Do-Re-Mi!

What Happens When It's over?

1. How to answer questions

So, even after you have finished giving your presentation, it isn't actually over yet. Chances are that you are going to have to answer some questions from the audience. As your presentation was clear and concise, people may have some specific questions regarding theories you may have used or the future relevance of your presentation. In this case, it is important to prepare for everything. It's kind of like arriving early for your presentation. You have to make sure there will be no surprises. Plus, you should already have a broad understanding of the topic at hand so you will most likely know how to answer the questions. It's just about answering them in the clearest and most effective way.

To begin, you should prepare at least ten possible questions and points of interest that the audience may have. In case someone asks a question for which you did not prepare, relax, and breathe through it. You are allowed to take your time. You are also allowed to say that you don't know something. A good response to this kind of situation is, "I am unsure of that specific notion (or concept, or question) at this point in time, but come see me after the show and we can discuss it." This is a good way to build connections because you can exchange contact details and answer the question. If you don't want to do this, then you may also respectfully decline by saying, "I will double-check that at the next available moment." Either way, if you don't know the answer, don't be afraid to say so. You might come off worse if you pretend you know what you are talking about.

That being said, always remember to be kind and courteous to your audience. There are potential connections and opportunities sitting right in front of you and it would be a shame to have all your hard work go to waste.

2. Network

As I said, the audience is full of opportunity and meeting the right person at the right time could change your life. That is, if you give a good presentation. Remember to bring some business cards or just provide an email or number by which people can contact you. In this day and age, knowing the right people can get you very far.

The key thing to remember when networking is always to remember the names of the people you meet. If you are bad at remembering names, say them out loud. It means a lot to people when you remember them and it's an easy way to make yourself stand out.

Networking can also do wonders for your public speaking confidence, just like meeting the audience before your presentation, except now you can relax and enjoy their company.

3. Let it simmer

It might seem like the right thing to do, but going home and immediately picking apart your speech is not a great idea. You have probably spent weeks preparing for your presentation, working through your anxiety, and building your confidence. You just gave the presentation and all of the build-up you experienced on that day alone is enough to make anyone want to take a nap. You have worked hard and came a long way and you are probably feeling proud of yourself. So bask in that feeling for a while. Give yourself a few days before you decide to identify what you did right and what you did wrong. It's kind of like when you are making bread. When you start kneading the dough, it feels tight and strained. However, if you knead the dough for a few minutes and let it rest before kneading it again, you will notice the dough is softer and more elastic. This is because, while the kneading part of the process is vital to making great bread, so is not kneading. When you rest it, the dough has a chance to build up gluten fibers (which is what makes it elastic). So let yourself rest, and let all that information sit there and simmer. When you revisit the presentation, you will be able to look at it with fresh and kind eyes.

4. Assessing your performance

You have let yourself simmer and now you are ready to assess your performance. People tend to go one of two ways here. They are either extremely excited and confident in their performance and see nothing that can be improved upon, or they crawl up into a ball of self-loathing and pity and can't find a single positive thing about it. Ideally, we want to be in between these mindsets. On one hand, it's great to be able to notice that you did a great job; however, you still need to be able to improve on your performance. No one is perfect and there will always be something you can tweak or change. On the other hand, wallowing in self-pity won't make building your confidence for the next presentation very easy. It probably also is not a very accurate view of your presentation. You had to have done something right.

Try to be as honest as possible. Perhaps someone you know was watching and you can ask them for some advice. Generally, you will know what you did well and what could have been better. Perhaps you could have added one less pause or changed the punchline to a joke. It's called work-shopping and you are going to do it for the rest of your life, not just for public speaking.

5. Setting new goals

Let's say your goal for this presentation was just to get up in front of the audience and say your speech. Sure, the bar is not very high, but you are just starting out, so it's an acceptable first goal. However, if this is your goal every time, then you probably won't be improving very rapidly, or at all. You got through the presentation, so tick off that goal and start the next one. It may be to incorporate a joke or story into your speech. Perhaps you want to work on your intonation or body language. Maybe you need to be more emotive. Think of it like a board game. If your goal is the same every time you present, then you will essentially remain on the starting block forever. But once you start to set new goals and fulfill them, you can move onto the other blocks and eventually make it to the finish line.

It's not just about the presentation, it's about everything that comes before and after it as well. So, make sure you are prepared and most of all, make sure you have fun!

Chapter 8:

How to Effectively Deliver Your Speech

Throughout this book, we have touched on the concepts of intonation, cadence, suspense, body language, and presenting yourself. I have decided to give these elements a chapter of their own for a deeper discussion because they are essential to the delivery of a captivating and informative presentation. The Greeks believed that great content was not enough; rhetoric was also about how the content was delivered and if either one of those elements was lacking, the communication would also be ineffective. I know I said that if you are feeling nervous, you don't need to worry about how you deliver the speech; just try to get the information out. But this advice is a mere stepping stone in the rest of your public speaking journey. Once you have presented for the first time and know that you can actually do it, it's time to fine-tune your skills and ensure that the way you deliver your presentation is just as developed as the presentation itself.

We might think that, when we feel nervous in front of the audience, we are the only one who can feel it. But the audience is more intuitive than we would care to admit. They pick up on your signals, the shaking of your hands, the sweat dripping down the side of your face, and the slight stammer you picked up at the start of the presentation. They feel all of the nervous energy and it makes them nervous and uncomfortable as well. Once they start to feel uncomfortable, that's all they can pay attention to and it doesn't matter what you are saying anymore—they just don't want you to pass out! Using verbal, non-verbal communication, and body language to communicate to the audience that you are confident and comfortable will put them at ease and allow them to truly take in what you are saying. Sure, we covered how to boost your confidence and overcome your fear and anxiety previously, but for these accomplishments to come across, the audience has to see it in action.

Verbal and Non-Verbal Communication

Verbal communication refers to the transmission of information using your voice. Non-verbal communication refers to the transmission of information with everything but your voice, like your body, facial expressions, eye contact, gestures, and stance. The effect of tone falls somewhere in between these concepts. Will Smith's character, Alex Hitchens, in the movie *Hitch* (2005), identifies the importance of non-verbal communication stating, "60% of all human communication is non-verbal body language; 30% is your tone, so that means 90% of what you're saying ain't coming out of your mouth." While what you say is important in terms of your credibility and getting your message across, the audience will be more responsive to your visual cues and non-verbal communication which is why perfecting your delivery can improve your public speaking success astronomically.

A great place to start is by looking at other people. These people do not necessarily have to be speaking publicly or performing in front of an audience; they just need to be speaking. Watch how your friends use their bodies and facial expressions to tell a story. Do they stand dead still with a blank face speaking in the same tone with their arms tightly fixed to their sides? If that's how they tell a story, then even though their story might be interesting, it's going to seem like the most boring one ever told. Similarly to your presentation, if you just stand there, your audience won't be able to make a connection with you. It's like building up a giant wall and speaking from behind it. Unless you are Pink Floyd, it's probably not going to work.

Like finding your voice, you also have to find your body language. And you guessed it, you can do this through a healthy dose of introspection. Try to be aware of your body language when you are in a comfortable situation. Watch what you do when you tell a story. Does your face move in a specific way? What do you do with your arms? How are you standing? Do you speak loudly and expressively or is your description dry? It defeats the point to be conscious of yourself when you are trying to decipher your subconscious motions and ways of being, but this can help you find the most natural and comfortable way to express yourself.

Another way to figure out how you naturally speak and express yourself is to make a recording. You can do this in one of two ways. Firstly, you can just record yourself telling a story to the camera. You will be able to see our movements and facial expressions and even double-check your content while you're there. Secondly, you can ask your friends to surprise you with a hidden camera one day. You won't know when or where the camera will be recording and in this way, you will get an accurate idea of how you express yourself. Practicing in front of the mirror is also an effective way to judge how you use your body when speaking. It allows you to see when something looks unnatural or wrong. Let loose and try a few different movements to get a feel of what looks natural and confident and what doesn't.

Like with your voice, you don't have to change it or pretend to be someone else. All we are doing here is working with what you have and enriching it. Your unique rhythm is what will set you apart from every other person and you should embrace that. But it doesn't mean that we can't tweak you a little.

Verbal communication

Once you have found your voice, you can begin to learn how to use it effectively. It's not just about what you say, but it's also about how you say it. Audiences respond to more than just information and if 30% of your communication is influenced by your tone, then using this to captivate your audience further will help you to effectively relay your message to them.

1. What are you saying?

A quick recap: What you are communicating with the audience about is the essence of public speaking. To make this possible, you have to combine many other factors so that the audience can understand you. You will figure out what you have to say by researching your topic widely and preparing your speech accordingly. Remember the three-point format and keep it clear and concise. This will allow you to add more emphasis to the points you have made, instead of bombarding the audience with information. It is better to have three well-thought-out, developed and clear points than twenty vague and misleading points. So, once you have figured out what you are going to say, let's figure out how you are going to say it.

When you are delivering a presentation, it is important to avoid taking up space with "uhms" and "ahs." Uttering these fillers is an easy habit to pick up, but not a good one. These sounds do not add to your presentation in any way and should be avoided at all costs. While you practice your presentation, every time you say "uhm" or "ah," restart your speech until you no longer use these filler words. Do not replace these sounds with other filler words because the audience will notice it and they might end up fixating on it. Were you ever in a class and the teacher said "you know" or "right" before and after each sentence? Did you and your friends place bets to see how many times the teacher would repeat these phrases? You probably didn't learn much in those lessons. That was because it can be distracting and jarring to hear the same sound or phrase over and over again. If you have to replace it with something, try to tap your foot or move your finger lightly when you feel the urge to "uhm," but hopefully, you will have practiced it out of your system before the big presentation. If you are struggling to do it alone, there is an app called "Speeko - Public Speaking Coach" which helps you to track your use of filler words so that you can see where and how you need to eliminate them.

   2. Tone

Tone refers to how you say what you want to say. If someone is talking about how they won a race this past weekend, but they are saying it in an angry tone, then you might deduce that they aren't happy with their win. Similarly, if you are very upset about something that happened, but your tone is not expressive of that, the people around you might not understand that you are angry. Tone can sometimes feel like a vague, obscure concept that you can't really explain. Have you ever had a fight with one of your friends and they say, "It's not what you said. It was the tone you used"? You might find yourself confused by this statement wondering how they could have misinterpreted your meaning so grossly. This is because tone is an indicator of both emotion and state of mind. It is how your audience can determine when you are being sarcastic, when they should laugh, and when they should listen closely. Your tone is the map that guides the audience through the presentation. If your map tells you to go left every time you should be going right, then you will undoubtedly get lost. Similarly, if you speak in an angry tone when you should sound optimistic, your audience will not be able to interpret your meaning and the purpose of your speech will be lost on them.

If you are at work, a friendly and professional tone will be best suited to your presentation. Perhaps, if you are reprimanding your employees, a more serious tone should be used. If you are giving a presentation at school, then you can take on a more casual tone, while presenting at a social event may require a more jovial and relaxed tone. Think of tone like emotions. How do you sound when you are happy, sad, angry, anxious, worried, or excited? Ask yourself what emotions you want to evoke with your presentation and use tone to express them.

3. Enunciation

Too often, our messages have been lost in a jumble of words because we didn't know how to enunciate properly. Perhaps when speaking casually and with your friends and family, it is not essential to enunciate and pronounce all of your words correctly. But when you are speaking in front of people who have never heard you, they may find it difficult to understand you because they may not be familiar with the way that you speak, the rhythm you use, or how you pronounce words. To avoid this confusion, enunciating your words will allow the audience to understand exactly what you are saying. They won't have to contemplate what you were trying to say in a previous sentence and miss your next few sentences. If you are speaking from your diaphragm and your posture is open, articulating words will be easier. Open your mouth wide when saying every single word during the first few times you practice your presentation and when you feel like you've got it, then try saying the words properly with your mouth in a more natural position. Practice is key when it comes to enunciation.

Tongue twisters can be helpful when learning how to enunciate. For instance, if you know you struggle with "sh" sounds or "th" sounds good tongue twisters would be:

- Sheila shucks shells at the seashore.
- Thelma thought that thick thickets throw thorns.

Ideally, you will want the tongue twister to be short and simple. It's not really about the content of the sentence, but it's more about perfecting the sounds. Start slow and over-exaggerate your mouth movements when pronouncing the words. As you start to pronounce them clearer and clearer, you can start to say them faster. It also helps to watch videos of other public speakers and look for how they pronounce, articulate, and enunciate their words. Your content may be clear and concise, but for that to translate, you also have to speak clearly and concisely.

4. Projection

Okay, you know what you are going to say, you know how to say it, and you know how to say it right, but none of this matters if you don't speak loud enough for the audience to hear you. Speaking louder can feel draining and difficult for the majority of us. How we admire people who can use their voices to ask for things from across the room, seemingly effortlessly! You no longer have to be envious because projecting your voice can seem like the easiest thing in the world. You actually already know how to do it.

Stand up straight and breathe through your diaphragm. This will open up your lungs and allow more air to pass through your vocal cords, thus projecting more sound from your mouth. Remember the gramophone? Picture the air as the volume button. The more air you can push through your vocal cords, the louder you will speak.

You can also train yourself to speak louder. When you are practicing, make a point of speaking at a higher volume—perhaps higher than necessary—so that when you speak at the appropriate volume, it feels more natural. Try taking into account the size of the place you will be speaking in. Will you be presenting indoors or outdoors. Will you have a microphone? You will have to speak louder in larger auditoriums and outdoor venues than in a smaller conference room or classroom. If you have a microphone, then you will be happy to know that you can maintain a regular and comfortable volume, but you will need to pay extra attention to your articulation as microphones are not forgiving in this respect.

5. Pause

While pauses do not technically count as verbal communication, they are considered to be part of this grouping of verbal elements. This is because they are used within a sentence itself or between sentences. Pauses can be highly effective in drawing focus upon what you are saying and creating suspense. Think of your speech like an episode of a series. Something dramatic almost happens. For example, a bomb is about to explode in the protagonist's house. You are on the edge of your seat, and time doesn't matter. All that matters is what is about to happen next and suddenly, the credits begin to roll. Your head rolls back and you let out a groan of despair. The suspense is enough to drive you crazy. Similarly, a pause can create suspense for your audience. If you can incorporate a few useful pauses in your presentation, then not only will the audience be focusing on what you are saying, but their focus will also be maintained.

A good time to incorporate a pause would be after a rhetorical question. This gives the audience some time to think about the answer as they wait for you to clarify the answer for them. You can use a pause right before the climax of your story or joke. Think of it like this: Have you ever been so hungry that all you can think of is food? You picture a delicious, home-cooked meal accompanied by your favorite dessert and a glass of red wine. The food seemingly melts in your mouth as you devour it quickly and without mercy. But when you actually start eating, you quickly feel full and it should feel good, but the promise of a delicious meal was almost better than the meal itself. This is the type of way that the audience can feel when you put in a suspenseful pause. Sure, they will be satisfied with the information, but it will be the suspense that really gets them going, the tension created that really draws them in and makes them want to know more.

Pauses allow the audience to simmer in their own curiosity. Similarly to how hearing stories can cause the body's endocrine system to release small amounts of cortisol, a pause can foster a slightly stressed atmosphere for the audience. Use this stress to your advantage and lead the audience where you want them to go. Dangle them by a thread and catch them with your safety net of information.

6. Pace

Presenting is not a race. It's not about who can finish their speech faster. You don't get a medal for being fast. On the contrary. Think about how, at the end of certain medical advertisements, where they quickly list all of the side effects of the medication being advertised. Can you remember a single one of those side effects? Probably not. Pace is your friend. It can be used to guide the audience through your presentation or it can put unnecessary strain and pressure onto your audience.

If you try to get through a ten-minute presentation in under five minutes, a lot of the meaning in your speech will be lost. Speaking quickly can also affect your articulation and enunciation, making it even harder for the audience to understand and grasp what you are telling them. If you speak at a painfully slow pace for the entire presentation, then your audience might start to feel bored and frustrated.

Mixing up the pace in your presentation will keep things interesting and force the audience to be on their toes. When you really want the audience to pay close attention to you, speaking slowly can draw them into what you are saying and once you have their undivided attention, you can speed it back up again. Using pace to transition into the next point is also effective as it acts as a sort of paragraph. The audience can't see the paragraph, so they have to get their cues from you, the presenter.

Imagine that you are telling the audience a funny story about a tremendously anxious person who you recently encountered. Merely describing this person as anxious does not carry much meaning to the audience. However, if you quicken your pace and use body language to express that the person was anxious, it will be more relatable and perhaps comical for the audience. Transport them to experience the situation with your use of pace and make them feel like they are there witnessing the story unfolding right before their eyes.

Non-Verbal Communication

1. Gesture

Gestures can be your best friend or your worst enemy in public speaking. Have you ever been to a speech where the presenter was waving their hands in the air every chance they got? Their movements were exaggerated and comical. When you are giving a speech about endangered animals, you probably don't want people to laugh at your gestures. However, you can use big gestures to grab the audience's attention and allude to the immensity of the problem at hand. Gestures are like the marshmallows in Lucky Charms cereal; delicious and novel, but if you have too many of them, the excitement is gone. A few gestures that you can use during your presentation might look like this:

- If you are asking a rhetorical question, then you can shrug your shoulders to make it look as though you don't know the answer. This form of gesturing is used comedically and emotively. Say, for instance, you ask the audience if they have ever cut someone off in traffic. When you answer that you have also cut someone off, then you can point to yourself to animate your statement.
- If you really do not know where to put your hands, then I suggest bending your arms at the elbows and joining your fingers so that your hands are in front of your body, in-line with your belly button. This makes it easier for you to perform other hand gestures and it also makes you seem more approachable as it is a passive stance. Plus, it does not look as strange as having your arms dangling awkwardly at your sides.
- If you want to demonstrate something to the audience like pressing a button or pouring a glass of milk, then you can make these motions with your hands. This can be particularly useful when telling a story or if you are giving a demonstrative speech.

Use your hands openly and comfortably. The audience will be able to tell if you feel awkward or do not know what to do with your hands, especially when you are speaking in a more informal setting. Try not to point, as this can come off as aggressive and may cause the audience to shut down instead of listening to you. However, if you are telling a particular story and a pointed finger is applicable, then by all means, do it. Gestures, like tone and pace, are used to make your presentation better and to carry information to the audience in a nicely wrapped package.

2. Stance

How you stand says a lot about your demeanor. If you walk onto the stage hunched over with crossed arms, the audience is going to assume that you don't want to be there. They will feed off this energy and struggle to listen to what you have to say. However, if you have a powerful stance, where your legs are shoulder-width apart, your arms fall confidently at your side, your chest is puffed out, and your head is held high, the audience will understand that you are in control and that you are the best person for the job.

Don't start your speech with a powerful stance and then slowly morph into a small turtle as your presentation continues. You want your audience to trust you for the ten minutes that you have their attention. Allow them to have confidence in you, and your presentation will be a success. If you are giving a presentation at work, no matter how comfortable you are with your colleagues, do not stay seated to give your presentation. Show them that you are energized and dedicated and that you are an authority of the topic at hand.

3. Eye contact

This is a big one. If you make eye contact with your audience, they will be able to see that you are engaging with them. Making eye contact will help you to build rapport with your audience and vice versa. Are you familiar with the cliché, *your eyes are the windows to your soul*? I'm not saying that I am in agreement with the phrase, but will suggest that they definitely have an impact on how people perceive you. If you have ever had pets, you know that when your dog has done something wrong or eaten something they weren't supposed to, they will avoid making eye contact with you. Humans do the same. There have been studies that discovered a way to determine whether someone is lying by looking at their eye movements (Steinhilber, 2017). If you have shifty, darting eyes, then you could be lying. So, trusting that you aren't lying, if you spend your entire presentation avoiding the audience, they might begin to question your character and credibility as a presenter.

4. Facial expression

If someone looks at you and says *yes* with a sour face while shaking their head from side to side, you probably won't be very confident in their answer. Similarly, if someone says *no*, but nods their head up and down, you will be confused. If your facial expressions and body language are in contrast to what you are telling them, then instead of listening to what you have to say, they will focus on why your expressions are not matching up.

Try to be animated, but not too over the top, because this will detract from your presentation. You aren't a clown, and this isn't a performance, but you still need to maintain a level of expression that enhances what you are saying. Even if you are at work, professionalism does not mean that you have to keep a straight face throughout the entire presentation. If you want to engage your colleagues, you can show them with your gestures and facial expressions that the business has grown five percent in the most recent quarter. Point to your slides and use gestures to animate them. Use your hands to show when something has increased or decreased and use a smile to motivate your audience.

5. Space

If you are standing on a gigantic stage in front of thousands of people and you only use one square inch of the stage to stand on, you are doing it wrong. Have you ever seen Beyoncé or Lady Gaga use only a tiny portion of the stage? Sure, maybe when they are singing a ballad, but during the whole of the performance, they make use of the entire stage to entertain the audience. You don't have to walk the entire surface of the 20-meter stage because you might end up wearing yourself out and it would probably just look silly. However, you do have to use a large portion of it. Try to walk back and forth towards the audience to grab their attention. Maybe if you are telling a story and you whisper for effect, walk right up to the edge of the stage and pretend that you are whispering in the audience's ear. Give yourself space to express yourself to maintain the audience's focus. If you are giving a speech in a small conference room or classroom, then you might not have much room to move around. You can still create the illusion of space with your hand gestures and stance. Sometimes creating space can be just as important as taking up space in a physical sense. Think of it like a pause. Space gives you and the audience a chance to breathe.

Dress for the Part

Remember, the audience's perception of you is linked to how well they will engage with the information you are sharing. If you walk out in front of them, un-showered, wearing beach shorts and a loose, unbuttoned shirt, they probably won't take you seriously. You aren't going to the beach; you are giving a presentation, and you should dress that way. Similarly to how it is important to prepare a presentation with a specific context in mind, it is important to dress for a specific context. At work, you will need to look professional and clean while at school, you might be able to get away with something more casual. If you look too dapper, this could also distract the audience.

When in doubt, wear darker colors. If you wear bright pink pants with an obnoxious polka dot shirt, the audience will be focused on your outfit instead of what you have to say. Darker colors will allow them to concentrate on your presentation. You want to stimulate the audience in the right way, not overwhelm them with your fashion choices. However, context is important because if your presentation asks for it, your outfit might actually benefit you (depending on the topic you are communicating). If your bright pink outfit is going to help you in the long run, then wear it. In most cases, it is advised to stick to black or navy blue. Similarly to how Apple markets its products on a white background, you need to market your information on a plain background.

If you wear makeup, try to follow the same rule of thumb here. Make sure the makeup is understated and neutral. Try to avoid bright pink, red, orange, or maroon shades because they can be distracting. While you may look amazing and feel confident, the goal here is to grab the audience's attention and maintain it (for the right reasons). You want the information to grab their attention, not your red lipstick. However, if you are performing on a big stage in an auditorium in front of a lot of people, then wearing a little more makeup than usual can benefit you. This is because the audience is very far away and they won't be able to see the make-up on your face, but it will make your face look flawless. Guys, don't be shy to wear some foundation and concealer. You want the audience to look at you and think, "Wow, this person has got their stuff together, so I am going to listen to them."

If you wear reading glasses, wear them for your presentation. A study has alluded to the fact that glasses can make you appear more intelligent and competent (Halliston, 2013). While this tip is not 100% foolproof, it does give some insight into the audience's perception tendencies. Basically, the audience will listen to you if you look professional and put-together. You may not want to wear glasses, but if you can curate the rest of your outfit to portray a sense of confidence, then you are good to go.

Not only does dressing for the part have an influence on your audience, but it will also have an influence on your confidence. We have all been there. You buy yourself a new suit or dress and all you want to do is wear it. You put it on and suddenly you feel as if you are on the runways of Paris, all eyes on you, strutting your stuff. This kind of confidence will show when you step out in front of your audience and should be embraced at all costs. So, wear something that makes you feel amazing and keep your context in mind. You don't really want to show up in an evening gown or tuxedo for your monthly sales update. But do wear something that makes you stand a little taller and talk a little prouder.

If you aren't comfortable, then the audience will realize this. So, even though those heels might make you look taller, your discomfort would not be worth the sacrifice. Sure, tight suits might be trendy and fashionable, but if you can't lift your arm to gesture to your slides or end up waddling on and off the stage, your audience won't be able to take you seriously. It's like running a marathon. You might look cute in your frilly latex suit, but it really is not a practical option for running long distances. Be context-specific and make sure you dress comfortably.

Sometimes, you might want to spice up your outfit with some jewelry and accessories. You might look great, but you have to remember that accessories can be noisy. If you are wearing ten sparkly gold bracelets on your arm, then every time you move your hand up to gesture or point, it will sound like Santa is coming to town. Be cognizant of how your accessories sound and whether they are overpowering your general outfit. Celebrated fashion designer Coco Chanel once said, "Before you leave the house, look in the mirror and take one thing off." or in the case of the bracelets, take ten off.

In the same breath, accessories can be distracting if they are too big. Do not wear a hat because this will obstruct your face. On a practical note, the audience will not be able to see your facial expressions and eye contact could be difficult in this case. If the audience cannot see your eyes, then they may assume that your character is dubious and this could bring your credibility into question. Also, make sure your hair is not in your face. You want the audience to see you, so that they can build rapport with you to take in what you are saying to them.

While it is unfortunate that humans attribute so much importance to the way other humans look, we are a visually stimulated people and using this to your advantage will help you in the long run. It would be great if we could all look exactly how we wanted to and still have people listen to us because what actually matters is what we say. But until that day comes, wear darker colors, try to look put-together and add some of your unique flair to your appearance. At least you will slowly be changing public opinion instead of pushing change upon your audience. They will appreciate you for it, even if they don't know it.

Part 4: Keeping Your Presentation Interesting

Chapter 9:

How to Use Technology to Boost Your Presentation Skills

We live in a digital age where it can sometimes seem like our entire lives are being broadcasted online. We communicate online, we buy groceries online, and we work online. Sometimes one questions the need for any real physical interaction. While the modern age might seem overwhelmingly technological, we are still humans and human interaction is a vital part of our existence. We are not solitary creatures, although this doesn't mean that we can't use technology to enhance our presentations. Technology can be a valuable set of tools used to interact with other people. Instead of giving in to the extreme of a solely technological life, we can find a middle ground where technology and human interaction co-exist in a symbiotic relationship.

It can feel overwhelming to incorporate technology, slides, and graphics into your presentation. You might feel like you need a degree just to navigate your way through the platforms to create a presentation worth showing. Luckily, because technology has developed rapidly, so has the ease with which we use it. You don't have to have a master's degree in graphic design to create a captivating and interesting presentation because user interfaces are simple, clear, and guided.

This chapter will give you an idea of which platforms you should use to create your presentation while offering a helpful list of dos and don'ts. If you are ever in doubt or lacking some inspiration, you can watch the presentations of public speaking experts. Bill Gates gave a presentation about mosquitos and malaria and subsequently released a vat full of mosquitos into the auditorium. While this might be extreme, he did get people talking and that was, after all, the point. On a more basic level, watching how people use technology in their presentations will allow you to stay up to date with the latest trends and techniques. You don't really want to show up with a Clip Art presentation from 2005. Watching other presenters can keep you relevant and informed while giving you some inspiration for your own presentation.

Not sure where to look? TED Talks has become the world's most famous public speaking platform. Plus, they showcase a wide variety of presentations. Some people use slides, and others don't. Some release mosquitos onto the audience. Either way, you will be able to learn a lot from the wide array of hosted presenters.

What Is Out There?

Finding a program that works for you is kind of like finding the right pair of shoes. Some look pretty, but end up hurting your feet. Others may be super-comfortable, but are dirty and tattered. The program that you decide on needs to be the perfect blend of functionality and style and it also needs to suit you and your lifestyle. So, let's get started with a few of the most popular and effective presenting programs available:

1. Keynote

Like all Apple products, their main focus is on functionality and ease of use. This user-friendly platform can be used on your mobile as well as on a tablet or desktop and because the Apple ecosystem is so integrated, moving the presentation between these mediums is but a button press away. This is also useful because you might be working on your desktop, but have to take the train to a meeting. You can continue to work on the presentation on your way to the meeting. You also won't need to worry about storing the presentation because it is always available on your phone or tablet. This will be very convenient on the day of your presentation. You won't need as many cables and hard drives to get your slides up and running.

Keynote allows you to start with an outline of your presentation and then flesh out the details. You can actually plan your entire speech and presentation on this platform. It also allows you to incorporate videos on the slides for an interactive audience experience. They have a variety of different themes you can choose from, making the process a little faster if you don't want to fiddle with too many design elements. However, their variety is not as wide as some presenting platforms. Often, placing images can be a labor-intensive part of creating a presentation, but Keynote allows you to drag and resize to your heart's content. If you are looking for a fast and easy platform on which to create your presentation, Keynote is the one for you.

2. Mighty Meeting

If you don't have Apple products, then you can use Mighty Meeting on your Android. However, you have to create the presentation first and then upload it onto Mighty Meeting which then allows you to present or annotate your presentation. While it is unfortunate that you cannot create the presentation itself on the platform, it is the perfect platform to use in classrooms. Students can annotate each other's presentations to make the learning process more interactive.

3. Google Slides

Google Slides is a great alternative to PowerPoint. If you have a Google account then Google Slides is free and allows other users to comment and annotate the presentation while it is happening. However, it does provide a rather limited selection of templates which means that you might find someone presenting in a similar style to you, especially in the classroom. If you are pressed for time and looking for a platform with which to create a quick and simple presentation, Google Slides is for you. While not as developed and flexible as Keynote and PowerPoint, it is still a useful and effective option for creating a presentation.

4. PowerPoint

PowerPoint is one of the most famous and popular presentation platforms in use today. This is mainly because Microsoft is so widely used, but also because it gets the job done. It has a wide range of stock photos, animations, fonts, and styles that you can choose from to make your presentation more entertaining. You can use templates or you can create your own design. Not that you will have to pay for some premium templates. Overall, PowerPoint is one of the best, most reliable, and most accessible platforms available.

5. Visme

The nice thing about Visme is that it makes animating your elements, like graphs and charts, simple and easy to produce. It also has a wide variety of templates and you can use Visme without any internet. This is the safety assurance you need in times of desperation. However, while Visme is a great option, you can only create a limited amount of presentations before you have to subscribe and pay for the program.

6. Canva

Canva is like PowerPoint's younger, prettier sister. It provides a wide range of templates, tools, design elements, and shapes to choose from for designing your presentation. It does come at a price, but once you have it, it is so worth it. Canva does a really great job at releasing new designs and images and uploading your own images is quick and easy. Plus, once they are there, you don't have to keep uploading them to each slide because they reside in your gallery. Additionally, Canva allows you to measure where you place your information and pictures ensuring that you can center and place these elements appropriately and accurately.

7. Prezi

Prezi is on the same level as Keynote and PowerPoint in terms of popularity and functionality. Unfortunately, Prezi's strongest selling point is also its weakest. It allows you to create non-linear presentations, meaning that you don't just have to move from slide to slide. For example, you can go into slides to find another section with more information (like a trap door) or move diagonally through your presentation. It can be fun and exciting for the audience, but it can also be overwhelming and exhausting, especially because you can only create non-linear presentations of Prezi. These may be novel elements to incorporate in parts of your presentation, but not throughout the whole thing.

8. AIO Remote

This tool does not allow you to create presentations; however, it will help you in front of your audience when you are delivering a speech. Whether you are presenting in front of a large or small audience, it can be distracting to have to either stand close to your computer or to run back to your computer to change the slides. If you find that you do not present on a regular basis, then investing in a clicker seems unnecessary. AIO Remote is an app that allows your phone to function as a clicker, so that you can move between slides effortlessly and seamlessly. You won't have a bulky laptop in your way and the audience will be able to see you clearly.

How to Keep Your Presentation Interesting

1. Plan it out and be consistent

While this might not be a tip to make your presentation interesting, it is a tip to keep it accurate and understandable. If you are introducing yourself, then showing the audience the slide that discusses your first point will be confusing and futile. Not only will it be irrelevant, but the audience will wonder why you and your slides are not synced, instead of listening to you.

When you start preparing for your speech, as you outline your introduction, body, and conclusion, you should already start planning out which slides you want to put in and where. Slides are there to enhance your presentation, not to overpower it or to act as a nice background image. A good rule of thumb is to show one slide per minute. If you are giving a ten-minute speech, then you should have no more than ten slides. Every time you move slides, the audience's attention refocuses to the new slide. If you do this too frequently or rapidly, they might feel like they are watching a tennis game. Keep it in order, match it up to what you are saying, and let the slides enhance your presentation.

2. Include a grand summary

This is similar to the conclusion you will be giving, as the audience needs to have a full and complete representation of what your presentation was about. This is a slide that you can leave on the screen for the last two to three minutes of your presentation to indicate to your audience that you will be signing off soon and to clarify any misunderstandings. If at any point during the presentation they got distracted or forgot to look at a slide, all of the information can be found there. This is also a useful thing to make available to the public, in case they were not able to attend. At work, a grand summary can help the employees to consolidate the meeting and leave with a full understanding of your message. At a social event, this may be unnecessary and instead of a grand summary, you can end with a selection of photos or a final statement. Most of the time, using slides at a social event will not likely be necessary.

3. Use animation

Don't worry, you didn't have to study animation to be able to add motion to still images. Apps like Canva and PowerPoint make this process simple and easy. For work presentations, animation can be a great way to show increases and decreases. If you have a table chart and want to show the company's growth or sales for the quarter, then animating the bars can refocus the audience to make the information more stimulating.

If you are presenting at school, this can be particularly useful to attract and maintain the attention of younger people as they tend to respond well to stimulation, change, and movement. Instead of making big gestures and striding across the classroom, the animations can do this for you. Yes, you still have to use body language, but it needn't be as exaggerated if you have an exciting presentation to back you up.

4. Have a great cover image

In an ideal world, delays would be a thing of the past. People would be punctual, nothing would go wrong, and you could give your speech on time. However, sometimes things do go wrong and people show up late and you may have to start your presentation a little bit later than expected. In this case, it can be valuable to have a striking, informative, and simple cover image for the audience to look at until you present.

Firstly, this image can give the audience an idea of what you will be discussing which allows them to enter into the correct mental space for your presentation. It also creates a level of curiosity that can be used to maintain the audience's attention throughout the speech. Secondly, it prevents the audience from getting bored while they wait for the presentation to start. The cover page can act as a conversation starter for the members in the audience. And if the wait is longer than expected, hopefully they won't notice as much because they will be occupied.

5. Use polls and live-action data

If the venue has the right equipment, including an internet connection, your audience can be a part of your presentation. On social media, people use polls to answer questions and engage with their audience. Well, the same can occur in a presentation. Ask the audience a question and tell them how to vote. Pull the data up toward the end of your point (as people will need time to register their opinions) and use the live data to impress the audience. Now, you do run the risk of distracting the audience for a minute; however, if done right, this can be an exciting refocusing technique as well. People will be intrigued by the idea of having their opinion matter to your presentation and will most likely return their attention to you as soon as they have cast their vote. Just be mindful that a poll should either be a simple yes or no question or a choice between two options. Overcomplicating this can lead to frustration for both you and the audience.

What Not to Do

1. Do not write your entire presentation on your slides

This might seem like a great idea to help the audience to stay on track, but it can be detrimental to your presentation. If there is too much information on your slides, the first thing that happens is your audience reads the slides and does not focus on what you are saying. Yes, they may get the gist of the presentation, but even though you worked so hard on your body language, tone, and articulation, the power of the message could be lost if they don't pay attention to you. You might as well have handed them a pamphlet with all of the relevant information instead of presenting it to them.

The second thing that happens is that your audience starts to feel overwhelmed and tired. Their brains oscillate between listening to you and reading the presentation and the overstimulation causes them to shut down.

2. Simple, but not too simple

Sometimes, for the sake of simplicity, we end up with a few obscure keywords on a page. This will be just as disruptive for your audience as having the whole presentation on the slides because it will leave them confused. As the presenter, you have to guide them. This would be like using a map that shows only landmarks and no roads, and would be highly ineffective in getting the audience where they need to go. Don't be scared to put information and sentences on your slides, but stick to a 60-40 proportion at all times; 60% space and 40% information on each slide. In this way, you can avoid over-cluttering and under-utilizing your slides.

The colors you use for the slides are important not only for the general aesthetic of your presentation, but also for the psychological effect that color can have on the audience. Ever wondered why McDonald's, KFC, and Burger King use the color red for their branding? That's because red has a sense of urgency attributed to it and it has been tested that yellow and red can induce feelings of hunger in people. Just like your outfit, stick to plain colors, although in this case, pastel colors are more effective than dark shades. This is because the darker colors can detract from the information on the slides. Try to use complementary colors as these are pleasing to the human eye. If you don't, your color choice could end up causing some discomfort for the audience and you wouldn't want something as basic as a color scheme to do that. Blues are always a great choice as they are professional and stable. Orange can be effective in focusing attention on a specific place and green is considered to be a *friendly* color. If you are giving a presentation on nature or a natural product, then beiges and greens will match the topic you are discussing. Color also requires you to be sensitive to the content and context of the situation.

3. Don't make it unnecessarily complicated

Okay, say you have the appropriate amount of information on your slides and they are all in the right order and timed out perfectly. At this point, you may notice a button on PowerPoint, or whichever presentation app you might be using. You see different options for animations and pictures and diagrams. Your head spins with excitement as you start to *dissolve* the title onto your cover page and give each main point a *boomerang* entrance, not to mention the *cascading* explanations. You want to stimulate the audience, but you don't want to overstimulate them to the point of confusion and exhaustion. Honestly, if you have animated graphs and charts, I would lose the entrance animations completely. It is outdated and unnecessary and will only succeed in distracting your audience or making your presentation look like an elementary school project. Keep it simple.

4. Don't try to be too relevant

Have you ever been to a presentation where someone tries to make a joke about youth culture using a popular meme, except they are two years late? If you are going to be relevant and up to date with the social trends of our rapidly changing times, then you have got to really be up to date. Find a young mentor to help to guide you through your presentation. Even if you are under 30 or over 60, having a young mentor can be just as significant as having an older one with more experience. If you want to make a joke, make sure people are going to find it funny. However, this also depends on your audience. Depending on their age range, it is useful to get some background information on the trends of their generation. Similarly, businesses market to Baby Boomers differently than they do to Millennials. If you want your presentation to be a success, then you have to take into account your audience, how they grew up, and what they respond to.

Chapter 10:
Public Speaking Pioneers

The world has known many amazing public speakers from Socrates and Aristotle, to Winston Churchill during World War II, to modern-day former President Barack Obama. There have been many in between and there will be many afterwards, but in this chapter, I will discuss three influential speakers of the 20th and 21st centuries. Each one of the speakers can teach you a specific lesson about public speaking, but to understand that lesson, we must first understand them.

1. Winston Churchill

Churchill came into power during a very tumultuous time for the Western world. War was breaking out, people were losing faith in their government, and they were not sure if they should join the war or let Hitler continue with his crimes against humanity. England needed a leader to guide them through this uncertain time and that leader was Winston Churchill.

At first, he was an unlikely candidate for public speaking because he had a speech impediment. This, of course, affected his speech and his confidence. However, after years of practice in politics and fine-tuning his speeches, he flourished as the public speaker England needed. He taught himself how to speak clearly and articulately so that people could understand him. His main aim was to boost the morale of his people and show the Germans that England was not afraid. He did this with a powerful and lively tone of voice and with his famous speech where he bolstered up support by stating:

> "We shall defend our island, whatever the cost may be. We shall fight on the beaches, we shall fight on the landing grounds, we shall fight in the fields and in the streets, we shall fight in the hills. We will never surrender!" (Churchill, 1940).

His use of repetition and short phrases got the audience excited, like a wave that starts small and gets bigger the closer it gets. He exclaimed at the end as a sign of solidarity and to hype up the audience, getting them ready for one of the most difficult times they would face.

Churchill is the perfect example of how important contextual relevance is in public speaking. Shortly after the war was won, Churchill was sworn out of power. This was because his aggressive tactics and morale boosting were particularly useful to a war-torn people, but not in the context of peace. He was such an effective speaker because he understood what the people needed to hear from him to get them through the war. He also understood that he had to show Germany that England wasn't going down without a fight. If he had adopted passive tactics and communicated with his audience indifferently and yieldingly, then the likelihood of victory would have been slim.

2. Maya Angelou

Angelou was an American writer, poet, activist, actress, and public speaker. Because of her background as a writer and novelist, she approached public speaking as another form of storytelling. She captivated audiences with her knack for rhythm and narrative. However, just like Churchill had battles to overcome, so did she. Angelou had a traumatic childhood which led to her stop speaking for five years. After this, she decided to use her voice for good and to inspire and uplift people. Angelou advocated and warned of the power of words. They can be used for good and evil and they can yield great influence.

Angelou's speeches were captivating, scintillating, and awe-inspiring. Because of her acting experience, she knew how to project her voice and articulate so the audience would know exactly what she was saying. She used her entire body and facial expressions to mimic the mood of her poetry or story or speech. She spoke at different paces, different volumes, laughed when the speech called for it, and paused at the perfect moments. She commanded an audience with her presence. Not only that, but what she was saying was just as significant, if not more, than how she was saying it. Her humanitarian work inspired women like Oprah Winfrey and Michelle Obama. She not only empowered herself through public speaking, but she empowered others. And that is the sign of a truly magnificent public speaker.

3. Barack Obama

Barack Obama is the former President of the United States of America who served his terms from 2009 to 2017. He is known as a compassionate, honest, and effective leader but, he is also admired for his light-hearted side. His speeches also reflected this. He would joke when it was necessary and was not afraid to laugh during his speeches. While he maintained a serious demeanor, the audience felt he was calm, collected, and relaxed.

Mr. Obama was not only the President of the United States, but he was also President of the pause. He never shied away from taking a small pause in the middle of his speech or sentence to gather himself and refocus the audience. Obama also used stories to help the audience relate to him and his vision of America. He spoke clearly and concisely and as the President of America, one is not only speaking to Americans, but speaking to the entire world. His public speaking abilities helped him to get elected for a second term and allowed him to motivate Americans to unite and find a common goal.

What Can We Learn and How Do We Implement Our New-Found Knowledge?

Barack Obama uses the technique of threes and repetition which can be highly effective in public speaking. In his inauguration speech, he started four consecutive paragraphs with the same *together, we* followed by a promise. This emphasis and repetition of togetherness and promise of the future gave the audience hope for his presidency. It gave the audience the sense that they, too, were a part of the running of the country and that together with Mr. Obama, they would lead

America and its people to success. Obviously, when you give your presentation you probably won't have as mighty a cause as leading a country to collective success. However, we can learn that incorporating your audience into your message can give them a sense of belonging and purpose. Ultimately, humans want to know why they are on this earth, and giving people a purpose is giving them a reason to live. Mr. Obama's use of threes and his repetition can be a useful tactic to employ in your call to action. Repetition not only reaffirms your message, but it can also act as a sort of crescendo moment that leads to the climax (the call to action).

Additionally, Mr. Obama teaches us about the usefulness and the power of pauses. He was not shy to take a three- or five-second pause (and neither was Maya Angelou). Those pauses created tension for the audience, they refocused their attention on what the presenter was saying and they gave time to the presenter to recollect their thoughts. You can use pauses for the same effect. The audience does not need to know that you are lost, yet they can merely think you are a skilled master of the pause.

From Maya Angelou, we can learn the importance of body language, facial expression, and intonation. Ms. Angelou was the Queen of verbal and non-verbal communication. When she got on a stage she was immediately the center of attention. She commanded the focus of the entire audience as she used her voice, intonation, pace and articulation to create an atmospheric, theatrical presentation. She used her entire body, stretched her arms wide and walked when she needed to walk. Watching her give a recorded presentation will show you how you can utilize these tools to give a captivating speech. She also seamlessly integrated stories into her presentations as they helped her to get her point across more effectively and interestingly.

Even though Winston Churchill was a speaker over 60 years ago, we can still learn a lot from him and his love for public speaking. Due to his speech impediment, he had to practice incessantly. He used to spend roughly one hour writing for every one minute of his speech (International Churchill Society, n.d.). On average, it would take him about ten hours to write a speech. So, the first thing you can learn from Mr. Churchill is how to persevere and strive for perfection. If you know your material, the rest will come easily.

Another thing you can learn from Mr. Churchill refers to his ability to speak to the times. He was a leader in one of the toughest times for England and he managed to make the right decisions and save not only his own country, but also the Jewish German population. His speeches got the people of England riled up and ready to fight. In battle, morale is half the fight. Mr. Churchill taught us to be context-specific. If the times call for a strong, aggressive approach, then that is what you must give. Obviously, we live in different times, but if your work calls for a clear and professional presentation, then you are obliged to give one. The same applies to school and social presentations. Combining Mr. Obama's use of repetition and Mr. Churchill's vigor, your call to action can propel the audience forward, kind of like dropping Mentos into a bottle of soda.

As you know, you can learn public speaking from all the greats. You have encountered the Greeks and the Romans and they have taught about the use of structure and emotion. Mr. Obama, Ms. Angelou, and Mr. Churchill have shown you that practice, repetition, and body language are the keys to success. Find other inspirational public speakers to learn from them, and be inspired by them. In this day and age, knowledge is but a button away. Find your heroes and try to emulate them, but remember to be yourself. There will only ever be one of you.

Conclusion

At times, it may feel impossible. How will you get over your stage fright? How do you push the boundaries of an invisible zone? Your journey doesn't end here. Public speaking is a part of your life and in an ever-changing world, you are going to have to stay on top of things. You also need to make sure that you don't fall back into your old fearful ways, but in case you do, here is a quick public speaking crash course for your convenience. Use it as a booster shot when you are feeling low or confused.

While there are many elements to public speaking, there are a few that will propel you forward quickly and effortlessly, mainly:

1. Confidence
2. Context and audience
3. Content

These three C's will allow you to communicate effectively, appropriately, and accurately. Of course, delivery, preparation, intonation, and body language are all incredibly important to your public speaking journey and the success of it, but without these three elements, your presentation will be lackluster. If you don't trust in your abilities, getting up in front of an audience will be painful and nearly impossible. Without preparing a speech that is tailored to a specific context and audience, you will never be able to reach them, on an informative, intellectual, or emotional level. If your content is not reliable, informative, and researched, the audience will have no reason to trust you. Not having one of these three elements can make or break your speech. However, if your tone is slightly off, or you use the wrong word, or you forget to mention something, your speech can still be a success. So, if you are struggling to find a place to start in this detailed guide to public speaking, remember the three C's.

As you progress and find your voice, you will be able to feel more comfortable and natural in your public speaking ability. After a while, it won't feel like you have to try so hard and you will just be able to speak. You have lived on this earth for a while now and you have a fully-shaped personality, a set of likes and dislikes, a preferred manner of dressing, and your own unique way of expressing yourself. You aren't starting from square one, even though some days it may feel that way. Instead, introspection will make you aware of these things and allow you to incorporate them into your public speaking persona. This book is merely a guide to help you fine-tune what you already have.

If you are feeling nervous about your journey and anxiety plagues you at every corner, try to be patient with yourself. The more you practice and present, the better you will start to feel. Trust your journey and trust that all of your efforts will come to fruition. You might not be able to reap the benefits immediately, but one day, you will walk away from the audience and think to yourself, *that felt amazing*. Because we live in a fast-paced, output-based world, we can find it frustrating to be initially unspectacular at something. We want to pick up a guitar and immediately be able to play like Jimi Hendrix, or pick up a paintbrush and paint impressionist scenes like Claude Monet. Unfortunately, that is not how it works and we have to push through the initial *but I suck at this* until we start to see some improvement. No one who is truly great at something ever started with all of the required skills and knowledge. Being good at something takes work and practice. So, give yourself a break, and you will get there soon enough.

Public speaking will not only give you the ability to speak well in front of audiences, but its lessons and dogmas will permeate your very being. Being able to communicate effectively will give you the ability to express yourself and your mind in ways that you never imagined. You may find that people understand you better; not just what you say, but you as a person. Being able to feel confident in your public speaking abilities will allow you to feel confident in yourself holistically. Dealing with the anxiety of speaking in front of an audience will give you the tools you need to deal with anxiety in your daily life. Public speaking, on a holistic level, is about self-improvement and self-acceptance. This journey could be the thing that gives you enough confidence to tell a waiter when they get your order wrong or to make sure no one pushes in front of you at the grocery store line. And no, you don't have to be arrogant or rude in any of these cases; you merely have to communicate calmly and effectively. These are just small examples of how public speaking can impact your daily life. I am sure you will find many more positive ways in which public speaking can benefit you.

But, if you aren't quite there yet and you still need your training wheels, fear not, because you can always fall back on the three-point format. If you aren't feeling super-confident or secure in your ability, do the research, make sure you know the topic, and you have planned out exactly what you want to say and say it. Faking it until you make it might seem counterintuitive or false, but if you can pretend to have confidence, eventually your brain will believe it. If you can back yourself up with the right content, then half the battle is fought. Delivery and confidence can come later to combine with your speech to form a super speech that captivates any audience.

It is also important to remember that you might not always be on a stage. Sometimes you will present in a small room or on a video call. Just because you aren't propped on a giant stage in a massive auditorium, does not mean that you are not speaking in public in the traditional sense. You still have to work on your confidence, your preparation, and your delivery. You just might have to switch it up a little. The Greeks didn't wait for a stage before they could speak to an audience, so they found a comfortable rock and began proclaiming. So, instead of waiting for a stage or the setup you have pictured in your mind, find yourself a rock upon which you can perch for your public speaking journey. It does not have to be an actual rock, but rather a figurative rock. In this way, you can be comfortable no matter the setting, because in your mind you will be in the same place every time. Perhaps you want to speak on the beach or in a field. Manifesting a setting for yourself can help you to manage your fear and anxiety as well.

Another tip to avoid doubt and confusion is to think of the Greeks and their philosophy of *Ethos, Logos,* and *Pathos*. You can use these elements to guide your speeches and presentations. Ask yourself whether you are being honest. Does your speech make sense? Are you using the audience's emotions to further your cause? It has been a while since you had to do some introspection I am sure, but mastering the art of public speaking is going to require consistent introspection from your side. Whether that is in finding your voice, expanding your comfort zone, or maintaining your goals, you will have to check in with yourself regularly to foster and maintain your success. The audience might seem like this enigmatic presence that has the power to destroy or uplift you. In a sense, they are. However, the audience is also just a group of people who have varying opinions, lives, and stories. Picturing them all together can be overwhelming and scary, but focusing on a select few can help to bring your presentation full-circle. Use their stories and emotions to your advantage to truly make a change in your audience and the world.

While you might not always be on your own side, the audience is. Even before you have stepped in front of them, they are inclined to view you as a credible speaker; that is, unless you prove to be otherwise. Very rarely will they reject you before you have started the presentation. The trick is that their loyalty needs to be coddled and sustained. When in doubt, picture yourself as one of the audience members. Would you find a particular fact fun? Would you laugh at your joke? Would you walk away from the speech with a better understanding of the subject? Answering these questions by ourselves can be difficult. Try to think of the times that you were an audience member. What stood out for you? What made you feel good? What didn't work? Learning from the mistakes of others can be just as helpful as learning from our own mistakes. And remember, making mistakes is okay. Everyone does it. You are but a mere mortal. The difference between a successful person and a failure is whether they have learned from their mistakes or not. If you can't grow, adapt, change, and admit things to yourself, then you simply won't be successful. Do you know of any successful person who stagnated? No, because as soon as they did, you stopped hearing about them. Would Apple have been such a hugely successful business if they stopped at the iPod? No. Instead, they released several iPods because they were constantly trying to find ways to improve the previous product. Not only that, but they created iTunes. When that became outdated, they turned cellphones into multi-purpose gadgets that could play music using their Apple Music platform. So don't stop. Keep inventing and improving yourself, and you will be surprised how far you can go.

As every great speech must end with a call to action, I call you to start your public speaking journey. In the words of Maya Angelou (n.d.), "People will forget what you said, people will forget what you did, but people will never forget how you made them feel." With that in mind, use your newfound public speaking abilities to not only communicate effectively, but communicate honestly, openly, and deeply with your audience. Make them feel something. Let them walk away better for having listened to you. Approach them with kindness, generosity, and hope. Public speaking is an art because it is a tool to improve the world we live in. Use your voice to change and inspire. The world wants to hear what you have to say. Though you think you may not have much to contribute, your voice is necessary and wanted. So speak up! Let the world bear witness to your place in it. Take up space, and make yourself known. Humanity will be better for it.

Before you know it, you will be able to look back at your progress. You started your journey with shaky legs and sweaty palms, but now you walk onto that stage, your shoulders are broad, and your chest is puffed out. The light illuminates your face as you glance over the audience, proud and mighty. You know no fear. You know exactly what you are going to say and how you are going to say it. You thank the audience for listening and being there and you are grateful for their presence. You feel the excitement in your bones and cheeks as you get ready to utter your first, perfectly thought-out words. Your slides are in order and you have discarded your cue cards. You have prepared for this and you are confident in your ability. The preliminaries are over, the main event is about to begin. You've got this.

References

Allen, S. (n.d.). 7 Simple grounding techniques for calming down quickly. Dr. Sarah Allen. https://drsarahallen.com/7-ways-to-calm/

Angelou, M. (n.d.). Public speaking quotes top 20. The Institute of Public Speaking.https://www.instituteofpublicspeaking.com/top-20-public-speaking-quotes/

Castillo, S. (2014). Your brain shows how confident you are: How rats taught scientists a thing or two about confidence. Medical Daily. https://www.medicaldaily.com/your-brain-shows-how-confident-you-are-how-rats-taught-scientists-thing-or-two-about-303794

Chanel, C. (n.d.). Do as Coco did. Little Grey Matters. https://littlegreymatters.com/tag/before-you-walk-out-the-door-everyday-take-one-thing-off/

Churchill, W. (1940). Famous quotes and stories. International Churchill Society.https://winstonchurchill.org/resources/quotes/famous-quotations-and-stories/

Churchill, W. (n.d.). Public speaking quotes top 20. The Institute of Public Speaking.https://www.instituteofpublicspeaking.com/top-20-public-speaking-quotes/

Daly, J., Vangelisti, A. & Lawrence, S. (1988). Self-focused Attention and public speaking anxiety. *Person. Individ. Diff. 10*(8), 903-913.

DeCaro, P. (2011). The origins of public speaking. The Public Speaking Project. http://www.publicspeakingproject.org/origins.html

Ebersole, B. (2018). How does my voice work? Temple Health. https://www.templehealth.org/about/blog/how-does-my-voice-work

Franklin, B. (n.d.). Public speaking quotes top 20. The Institute of Public Speaking.https://www.instituteofpublicspeaking.com/top-20-public-speaking-quotes/

Gaiman, N. (n.d.). Neil Gaiman quotes. BrainyQuote.com. https://www.brainyquote.com/quotes/neil_gaiman_461447

Ginger Leadership Communications. (2016). Why Barack Obama will be remembered as one of the greatest speakers of all time. https://www.gingerleadershipcomms.com/article/why-barack-obama-will-be-remembered-as-one-of-the-greatest-speakers-of-all-time

Halber, D. (2018). Motivation: Why you do the things you do. BrainFacts.org.https://www.brainfacts.org/thinki

ng-sensing-and-behaving/learning-and-memory/2018/motivation-why-you-do-the-things-you-do-082818

Halliston, J. (2013). Can wearing eyeglasses really help you with your job interview? Work it Daily. https://www.workitdaily.com/job-interview-wearing-eyeglasses

Hitchens, A. (n.d.). The importance of non-verbal communication. Ethos3. https://www.ethos3.com/speaking-tips/the-importance-of-non-verbal-communication/

International Churchill Society. (n.d.). War leader. https://winstonchurchill.org/the-life-of-churchill/war-leader/

Obama, B. (2013). Inaugural address by President Barack Obama. Obama White House. https://obamawhitehouse.archives.gov/the-press-office/2013/01/21/inaugural-address-president-barack-obama

Pang, K. (2020). How to tell a story when public speaking. Communication Coach Alex Lyon. YouTube Video. https://www.youtube.com/watch?v=_wt9dWtDywg

Raj, T. (2017). The phenomenal woman and exceptional public speaker: Maya Angelou. Pep Talk India. https://www.peptalkindia.com/the-phenomenal-woman-and-exceptional-public-speaker-maya-angelou/

Saks, A. (2014). Public speaking quotes: Funny, inspiring insights for your presentation. Spark Presentations.
https://www.sparkpresentations.com/public-speaking-tips-presentation-quotes

Steinhilber, B. (2017). How to tell if someone is lying to you, according to researchers. NBC News.
https://www.nbcnews.com/better/health/how-tell-if-someone-lying-according-behavioral-experts-ncna786326

Tillfors, M., Furmark, T., Marteinsdottir, I. & Fredrikson, M. (2002). Cerebral blood flow during anticipations of public speaking in social phobia: A PET study. *Biol Psychiatry, 52,* 1113-1119.

The Toastmasters International. (2017). Organizing your speech.
https://www.toastmasters.org/Resources/Organizing-Your-Speech

Twain, M. (n.d.). Mark Twain quote on confidence. GoalCast.
https://www.goalcast.com/2018/07/16/confidence-quotes/04_confidence_quotes_quotes_a_man_cannot/

West, C. (2020). 18 Presentation apps and powerpoint alternatives for 2020. Visme. https://visme.co/blog/presentation-apps/

Whiteman, H. (2016). Training the brain to boost self-confidence. Medical News Today. https://www.medicalnewstoday.com/amp/articles/314777

www.ingramcontent.com/pod-product-compliance
Lightning Source LLC
Chambersburg PA
CBHW071833080526
44589CB00012B/1004